Pr...

"What C-Level executives read to keep their edge and make pivotal business decisions. Timeless classics for indispensable knowledge." - Richard Costello, Manager-Corporate Marketing Communication, General Electric (NYSE: GE)

"Want to know what the real leaders are thinking about now? It's in here." - Carl Ledbetter, SVP & CTO, Novell, Inc.

"Priceless wisdom from experts at applying technology in support of business objectives." - Frank Campagnoni, CTO, GE Global Exchange Services

"Unique insights into the way the experts think and the lessons they've learned from experience." - MT Rainey, Co-CEO, Young & Rubicam/Rainey Kelly Campbell Roalfe

"Unlike any other business book." - Bruce Keller, Partner, Debevoise & Plimpton

"The Inside the Minds series is a valuable probe into the thought, perspectives, and techniques of accomplished professionals. By taking a 50,000 foot view, the authors place their endeavors in a context rarely gleaned from text books or treatise." - Chuck Birenbaum, Partner, Thelen Reid & Priest

"A must read for anyone in the industry." - Dr. Chuck Lucier, Chief Growth Officer, Booz-Allen & Hamilton

"A must read for those who manage at the intersection of business and technology." - Frank Roney, General Manager, IBM

"A great way to see across the changing marketing landscape at a time of significant innovation." - David Kenny, Chairman & CEO, Digitas

"An incredible resource of information to help you develop outside-the-box..." - Rich Jernstedt, CEO, Golin/Harris International

"A snapshot of everything you need..." - Charles Koob, Co-Head of Litigation Department, Simpson Thacher & Bartlet

www.Aspatore.com

Aspatore Books is the largest and most exclusive publisher of C-Level executives (CEO, CFO, CTO, CMO, Partner) from the world's most respected companies. Aspatore annually publishes C-Level executives from over half the Global 500, top 250 professional services firms, law firms (MPs/Chairs), and other leading companies of all sizes. By focusing on publishing only C-Level executives, Aspatore provides professionals of all levels with proven business intelligence from industry insiders, rather than relying on the knowledge of unknown authors and analysts. Aspatore Books is committed to publishing a highly innovative line of business books, redefining and expanding the meaning of such books as indispensable resources for professionals of all levels. In addition to individual best-selling business titles, Aspatore Books publishes the following unique lines of business books: Inside the Minds, Business Bibles, Bigwig Briefs, C-Level Business Review (Quarterly), Book Binders, ExecRecs, and The C-Level Test, innovative resources for all professionals. Aspatore is a privately held company headquartered in Boston, Massachusetts, with employees around the world.

Inside the Minds

The critically acclaimed *Inside the Minds* series provides readers of all levels with proven business intelligence from C-Level executives (CEO, CFO, CTO, CMO, Partner) from the world's most respected companies. Each chapter is comparable to a white paper or essay and is a future-oriented look at where an industry/profession/topic is heading and the most important issues for future success. Each author has been carefully chosen through an exhaustive selection process by the *Inside the Minds* editorial board to write a chapter for this book. *Inside the Minds* was conceived in order to give readers actual insights into the leading minds of business executives worldwide. Because so few books or other publications are actually written by executives in industry, *Inside the Minds* presents an unprecedented look at various industries and professions never before available.

I N S I D E   T H E   M I N D S

Inside the Minds:
Venture Capital Exit Strategies

*Leading VCs on Exit Strategies for Entrepreneurs &
Management Teams – Including M&A, IPOs, & Other Options*

If you are a C-Level executive or partner interested in submitting a manuscript to the Aspatore editorial board, please email jason@aspatore.com. Include your book idea, your biography, and any additional pertinent information.

Published by Aspatore, Inc.

For corrections, company/title updates, comments or any other inquiries please email info@aspatore.com.

First Printing, 2004
10 9 8 7 6 5 4 3 2 1

ISBN 1-58762-040-5 Library of Congress Control Number: 2004105712

Inside the Minds Managing Editor, Laura Kearns, Edited by Michaela Falls, Proofread by Eddie Fournier, Cover design by Scott Rattray & Ian Mazie

Material in this book is for educational purposes only. This book is sold with the understanding that neither the authors nor the publisher are engaged in rendering medical, legal, accounting, investment, or any other professional service. For legal advice, please consult your personal lawyer.

This book is printed on acid free paper.

A special thanks to all the individuals who made this book possible.

The views expressed by the individuals in this book (or the individuals on the cover) do not necessarily reflect the views shared by the companies they are employed by (or the companies mentioned in this book). The employment status and affiliations of authors with the companies referenced are subject to change.

Inside the Minds:
Venture Capital Exit Strategies

*Leading VCs on Exit Strategies for Entrepreneurs &
Management Teams – Including M&A, IPOs, & Other Options*

<u>CONTENTS</u>

Maximizing Exit Opportunities

Michael Carus

General Partner & CFO
JVP

Timing the Exit

In venture capital, timing is everything. You can back the best company in the world, but that doesn't ensure market success. The goal of every venture capitalist is to find a great company and help it create solid financials, nurture its ability to execute against market opportunity and take on tough competitors. Timing an exit is not a simple process. But exit too soon or too late and you've lost your window of opportunity to really create a significant value. Venture capitalists are, among all the roles we play, excellent weathermen. From the very beginning, we're trying to read the charts and graphs of our trade to determine what the market will need, and pay for, often years before the technology will hit the market. At JVP, we are typically early-stage investors. Often companies we back have reached technological feasibility but have only just begun the process of creating the go-to-market strategy, market acceptance/adoption, and execution of the business model. That kind of prediction ability is most crucial for a successful exit.

As venture capitalists, we are analyzing exit strategies from the inception of our involvement with a company. Once it is evident to us and the capital markets that a company is positioned to take advantage of the public markets, exit planning will take place. At that point, the company will have proven its business model and be positioned for hyper-growth. Only when a company has experienced continuous growth in its top-line revenue, has obtained profitability, and the business is tracking to continue with its climb can significant value be created through an exit.

As with any mission, patience and planning are the key to success. Generally we believe that it takes three to five years to be positioned to maximize an exit opportunity. The opportunity to accelerate this timeframe can arise when a large player in the company's space desires to acquire the company in an attempt to ensure differentiation and proprietary market control. The timeline can also be dictated by the public market's desire for a particular solution and technology, leading to increased demand and the company's early overachievement in execution.

The worst possible time to attempt an exit is prior to achieving the goals needed to prove the full value of the company. During the information technology "bubble," many companies were brought to the public markets and were acquired well before they proved the viability and repeatability of their business models. Times have changed and investors are more cautious, so most exits will be pursued not only after proving a company's technological prowess, but also upon proof of execution. This proof comes in many forms, but most VCs' criteria include a great management team that employs a repeatable and profitable sales process, coupled with a profitable business model.

Like most life-changing decisions, consensus among the decision makers to exit "private life" is key. Buy-in from a combination of the board, the executives, the investors and bankers will create a significant signal to "The Street" that the company is a serious force to be reckoned with. Once the decision is made, it is imperative that all the members of your team function as just that – a team. A variety of key people are involved in the pursuit of an exit strategy. A word to the wise: use them. Leverage their talents, connections, knowledge and dedication to successfully guide your ship to success. Please see page 12 for the line-up.

The Team	
Venture Capitalists	Here to provide guidance to the company on all matters involving strategy, valuations, timing, and management. They also provide an expanded contact list...and let's not forget the cash.
CEO	"The Chief" must convince an acquirer or institutional investor that he or she is capable of leading the company to success. The CEO must be viewed as the individual with the vision, ability to execute, and bandwidth to manage the company through its next phase of growth and challenges.
CFO	Must have intimate command over the numbers and the business model. His/her interaction with investment bankers, LPs, "friends & family" or the acquirer's financial team can make or break the exit.
Board of Directors	These are the people with the ability to bring in the capital, make connections in the industry, and be seen as a credible, objective, "conflict of interest-free" body that will continue to guide the company and vouch for its ability to succeed.
VP Sales & Marketing and the CTO	These are two critical members of the management team. Keeping customers calm, contented and secure in the knowledge that their service will not falter throughout the transition is key. Customers are the reason this exit is happening. Ensure that these two important individuals convey the benefits of the change and the company's ongoing dedication to their customers' needs.

Exit Options

There are two typical ways for a venture capital firm to exit an investment: initial public offering (IPO) or merger and acquisition (M&A). An IPO is usually the right exit strategy when it is clear that the company can grow into a self-sustaining, independent leader in its space. For VCs, provided that we receive the fair and full value for a company and management can smoothly execute the transition, IPO and acquisition are equally good exit strategies. That said, there are pros and cons to both options.

IPO	M&A
Provides validation of the company	Offers validation of the product line and strategy
Investor & management reap benefit of liquidity based on lock-up arrangements	Investors and management reap the benefit of liqudity based on the type of sale (cash or stock) and related lock up arrangements
Capital for growth is available at best possible valuation	Have the benefit of a larger company's capital strategy
Additional capital for acquisitions	
Time drain on management	No road show diversion
Open kimono to competitors	Ability to keep strategy discrete
Lose "nimbleness" in the face of regulations & disclosure requirements	No need for added pain, cost and risk associated with being public
Increased scrutiny by investors	No public scrutiny

From the perspective of the company, the best option depends on whether the management can successfully transition to becoming a management team with the full scrutiny of the SEC, the reporting responsibilities to shareholders, and the larger implications of being in the public eye. In terms of the most profitable exit for the management team, that depends on their goals and the stipulations of the exit. An acquisition may entail staying on board with the acquiring entity for a stated duration, perhaps up to three years, however consolidation of the two companies may actually force certain members of the management team to leave the acquiring company.

Most entrepreneurs (and of course their VCs) are most interested in the cash-outs, and as soon as the word acquisition arises, management wants to know how much, how soon and how long before they can purchase that dream car. Cash-outs may take place in tranches that can last years, rather than in one lump sum, or sales of a technology product alone can result in one payment and shares for the investor, for example. However, in order to have a merger or acquisition, oftentimes management is required to withhold selling their shares for a period of time. This is to ensure the acquiring party that the selling parties are interested in the successful results and integration of the acquiring company.

In the case of an IPO, cash-outs work differently. An IPO is great as long as the company can prove its long-term independent value to the market. Even so, there are usually lock-up periods that prohibit the members of the management team from selling their shares before six months. Every company and every exit strategy is unique; our job is to help them elect the best decision path possible for the company and for our investors.

Option 1: IPO

In pursuing an IPO, we first meet with bankers and select the lead and syndicate. We prepare the company presentation, and then prepare and file the S-1. We determine if there are any selling shareholders. Management conducts a significant road show, with the support of analyst research coverage. We then subscribe the round to the institutional investors. If not a selling shareholder in the IPO, we sell shares or distribute shares in accordance with lock-up agreements.

The decision about how much of the company to sell to the public is based on a variety of factors, including the amount of money the company needs, the amount of public float that the underwriters deem appropriate for the stock, how desirable the company is to the investors, if it is oversubscribed, the dilution that the owners want to accept, and so on. We sell as much of the company to the public as necessary to provide funds for further growth, keeping in mind that we also want to create an opportunity for the company to have another form of currency in its stock for purposes of mergers and acquisitions and secondary offerings of stock.

In an IPO, all preferred shares are converted to common stock. This removes liquidation preferences. The options will continue to vest under the normal terms. Therefore, the value will be distributed commensurate with the ownership percentages. In an acquisition, the order in which value gets distributed to the shareholders is in accordance with the preferred shares liquidation preferences, which are determined by the preferred share purchase agreement. The options also create value in the order described in the liquidation preference stages. Sometimes there is a "carve-out" for the management options in an M&A as an incentive to complete the transaction.

During an IPO, management has a lock-up period that is usually a minimum of 180 days. After that, even if it is allowable, members of the management team need to be very cautious of disposal of their shares. Investors will wonder why they should own shares in a company when the management team is selling.

If the venture capitalists are not part of a selling shareholder group (assuming the underwriter does not want us to be a selling shareholder), they are often subject to the same lock-up provisions as the management team. However, venture capitalists typically negotiate a certain number of registrations for selling shares when they make an investment. An example of how this might work is as follows:

The shareholders of a company that have registration rights shall have the right, for five years from the IPO, to two (2) "demand registrations" of an underwritten public offering of their registerable securities by an underwriter acceptable to the company and the holders of a majority of the registerable securities being offered in such demand, at the Company's expense. Such "demand registrations" may be initiated by holders holding at least 40 percent of the registerable securities. Holders are also entitled to unlimited piggyback and S-3 registration rights (or the equivalent), at the company's expense. This is where other investors are registering shares with the SEC for sale. In the event of underwriter (banker) cutbacks, often the holders of the most recent registerable securities converted, in the event of a demand registration, be entitled to first register their shares prior to the registration of any other shares, on a pro-rata basis, and holders of registerable securities shall be entitled to register a minimum of 30 percent of the offering in the event of piggy back registrations.

Option 2: M&A

The M&A process begins with the search for one of the following: (a) a larger company in the space looking to expand in the company's market, (b) a competitor looking to expand its market presence, or (c) a strategic customer looking to protect differentiation.

Typically a company will be working with several strategic partners for a while prior to an acquisition opportunity arising. Usually we would look within those strategic partners for one that would be appropriate to approach as a potential buyer. It is a long process of working together with customers – where both companies can see the clear benefit – that usually leads to an M&A opportunity.

When considering an exit, the company should already have a general idea of a fair value for itself through comparison to other players in the space. Company valuations are based on a variety of factors, including an assessment of both public and private company comparables; data on multiples, growth rates, and such like for the sector and related markets; and data on exit values of related companies.

Additionally, the selling company should have a clear idea of the value to the buyer of synergies that will result from the acquisition. For example, the seller should examine how the acquisition will affect the buyer's ability to cut costs, gain profitability, increase the ease of delivery and support of the acquired solution to the customer, and add incremental revenue, as well as the acquirer's market value accretion from all of the above.

Many times it is best to use an M&A banker to help manage the sale process and ensure fair terms for the deal. A company will want to hire a banker that has deep knowledge of the sector and has had significant experience with doing deals in similar situations. Although no two deals are the same, the process for evaluation and negotiation is often the same. The banker will help the company and its investors determine the value that the company can likely achieve. The banker will also help the company assess the market and the various potential suitors for the company to establish a competitive environment for the sale. The banker should also act as the first line for the company in discussing the basic terms of what a deal would look like. This allows the company management to concentrate on running the business and creating a buffer for negotiation.

Worst-Case Scenarios

When a company runs out of cash, has no additional funding strategies, and is forced to sell, this is what is known as a "fire sale" situation. A company never wants to find itself in such a position. However, in such cases the company has no choice but to get the best offer available for its assets.

Ideally, a company will have realized well ahead of time that this situation is inevitable and will have undertaken a process to align itself with a larger player in the space. This partnership can deliver some value back to the shareholders in an acquisition of the company or its assets, thus adding to the market value of the company itself.

In the worst-case scenario, a company that cannot find a buyer has a few options. It can try to merge into a public shell, it can try to sell off pieces of itself or its assets, or it can go into bankruptcy protection and try to obtain a DIP (debtor in possession) loan to continue.

The decision on which route to take is dependent on the value of the company's non-cash assets and the potential for the company to emerge from the cash crisis with a viable business model.

A DIP loan can be used when the lender feels that the value of the assets can act as substantial collateral for the loan and the cash will allow the company to get back on track. Of course, the lenders will need to be compensated for the risk. Unless a company emerges with a very strong turn around, the likelihood of the equity holder receiving a return is low.

If the company has certain assets yet there is little hope to create a viable business model, the company will try to sell off its assets. In this case, the investors are hoping to recoup any percentage of their investment that they can.

Advice to Entrepreneurs

A company should not be built with the sole goal of an eventual exit. An exit is the natural result of building a fundamentally sound, useful, growing, and asset-rich company.

Sometimes entrepreneurs pursue an exit strategy too soon or have an inflated idea of the company value. Especially when it is the first time out for a new entrepreneur, there is a tendency to concentrate on the exit, neglect the day-to-day running of the business, fail on executing an exit and, in the process, reduce the value of the company for a successful exit.

To achieve a successful exit strategy, entrepreneurs must (a) create a knowledgeable and well-connected team to manage the company, (b) ensure a sizable market for the product, (c) differentiate their company through a unique technology and business model, (d) convey the long-term value of the company to shareholders, limited partners, and all parties concerned, and (e) ensure open communication with limited partners to let them know when their returns are expected.

Prior to joining JVP, Michael Carus amassed his operational expertise helping to grow some of today's leading technology companies. He employs this extensive experience with numerous JVP portfolio companies, directing them to focus their business models to meet the specific demands of their customers. Michael also sources new investment opportunities in the enterprise software sector and is responsible for the fund's financial activities. He is a board member with Bridgewave, Bristol, Cogent and TeleKnowledge and advisor to a number of companies in the JVP portfolio.

Prior to joining JVP, Michael served as the Executive Vice President, Chief Operating Officer and Chief Financial Officer at Fundtech

(Nasdaq: FNDT), a JPV I portfolio company. In addition to his various operating responsibilities, Michael managed the company's IPO, acquisitions and secondary offering raising $130 million. Through Michael's leadership, Fundtech grew from $3.5 million to approximately $50 million in sales through the company's U.S. and international offices. Previously, Michael held various senior management positions at Geotek Communications (Nasdaq: GOTK) and prior to this, he was a CPA and Manager of Business Assurance at Coopers and Lybrand.

Michael holds a degree from Ithaca College in New York.

The Role of the Venture Capitalist

James B. Murray Jr.
Managing Partner
Court Square Ventures

The Role of the VC in Exit Strategies

When pursuing an exit from a venture investment, the role of the VC can vary from little involvement to total control. Involvement most often depends on the position a VC holds in the capital table, which, in turn generally determines his position on the board of directors. In rare instances, we have been involved in investments where we held such a small percentage of the company that we had no seat on the board and had virtually no voice in an exit transaction.

The opposite end of the spectrum and usually the preferred position is when the VC is one of the larger investors in a company. In these situations, a VC may not only have a seat on the board, but he may have a controlling position by virtue of holding or controlling several seats. In these instances, it is not uncommon for key directors, often the largest investors, to take control of the exit process. Key board members deal with the investment bankers and the potential acquirers. They often negotiate everything.

Contrast the case of an IPO where the board or investors cannot dictate the outcome regardless of who controls the board. Most often the board will select the investment banking firm(s) that will conduct the offering. But, management must lead the IPO process. The purchasers of the stock will be investing in the future of the business, and they will want to see the management team that will be running the business after the IPO is over. They want to be convinced by the management team that the team and its business plan represent a good future investment. Thus, it is management that must lead an IPO exit.

Alternatively, if a larger competitor is acquiring the company, one can anticipate that some and perhaps most of management will be gone not long after the acquisition. Therefore, investors sometimes may not want management involved in M&A (mergers and acquisitions) negotiations because management's interests may not be entirely aligned with those of the shareholders. Furthermore, most CEOs have never done an M&A transaction. You may often get a better price or terms if experienced VC board members control an M&A exit transaction.

Also, if an M&A transaction is large enough, it is often helpful to have an investment banker involved. Some VC investors find that it helps to have an agent involved to assist in touting the attributes of the business. An investment banker may be perceived as a more independent voice on the issues of valuation or future prospects and can help convince a buyer where insiders may be less credible.

How an Exit Strategy Arises

Exits arise in many different ways. The first type of exit, an IPO, is on the whole an internally driven decision. The investors on the board assess their company and try to determine whether it is one that the public would want to own; and whether or not the markets are ripe for a successful offering. More than anything else, these are questions of corporate maturity and corporate size. In order to take a company public under ordinary market conditions, the firm has to be mature and have a sustainable stream of revenues. In fact, in 2004's market substantial revenues alone are not enough. To be a candidate for an IPO a company must be operating at a profit. There was a period of time in the late 1990s when pre-profitability companies went public. In fact, there were even a few extraordinary IPOs where companies without revenues went public. That is unlikely to happen again any time soon.

In addition to revenues and profits, a company's IPO prospects are likely to be determined by corporate size. An old rule of thumb dictated that $50 million in revenue was the minimum necessary to take a company public. That was a '90s number. My guess is that in the post "bubble" era the threshold is probably a good deal higher now, maybe $70 to $100 million in revenues. The arithmetic behind this rule of thumb is straightforward. A company's stock will be priced as a multiple of earnings. If pretax earnings are great, say 20 percent of revenues, and the market is giving comparable firms a price to earnings ratio of 10 then the multiples work like this: 20 percent of $50 million in revenue is $10 million of earnings. When multiplied by 10 this gives the company a $100 million market value. If you are going to sell 20 percent of the company to the public (which is about all one might reasonably expect to sell in an IPO) then this will result in a $20 million public offering. Now consider that the company is going to pay underwriters and investment banking fees that total a little over 7 percent of the offering. 7 percent of $20 million is $1.4 million. Fees of $1.5 million are probably the bare minimum that a company can reasonably expect to be attractive to a good investment banking firm, which drives the conclusion that a company considering an IPO must have more than $50 million in revenues in order to successfully navigate through the process.

Assuming this analytical process leads the investors on the board into considering their company's IPO prospects, this analysis should not be conclusive. They must also look at the external prospects – the state of the public markets. Very, very few companies could have done an IPO in 2002 or 2003. In fact, technology companies had no prospects whatsoever. At other times the markets might be open enough to permit an IPO but the pricing may be unfavorable. If an IPO prospect is in an industry sector that is currently unpopular, the board may often defer an offering until they can expect favorable pricing. But assuming the markets are receptive and pricing looks favorable, an IPO can be one of the best ways for a VC to create liquidity and realize profits.

In contrast to an IPO, M&A exits are as likely to be externally generated as internally generated. Producing products or selling services in a competitive marketplace sooner or later puts a company on the radar screens of both its competitors in the same business and larger companies that would like to get into that business. M&A transactions occur either because a competitor wants to add to their existing business or a larger aggregator of businesses makes a strategic decision to acquire a business in the field to add to their product line. In some instances, the acquirer may see the acquiree as an upcoming competitor and attempt to acquire while it is still a small business, before it starts costing them competitively. All of these are examples of externally generated M&A interest.

The M&A opportunity can be internally generated when a company encourages acquisition discussions as an exploratory gambit. Then if a potential acquirer expresses interest the company may attempt to get an auction going and drive up the acquisition price by soliciting other acquirers. In such situations an investment banking advisor can often be helpful.

When to Pursue an Exit

The board has the responsibility of deciding when to pursue an exit. Sometimes the management of the company will come to the board and report that they have been approached by another firm interested in an acquisition or merger. Sometimes a visionary CEO or management team will generate an unsolicited exit idea. More often than not, such planning comes up first at the board level. Most often it is the VC investors who are focused soonest on a company's exit strategy. VCs are the ones who must constantly keep their finger on the pulse of the business, monitoring developments to determine when an exit would be appropriate.

From the investor's perspective, the best time to pursue an exit is whenever the business can get the highest price relative to the risk of continued operations. VC investors must be alert to when the business is, relatively speaking, the most valuable. As this is written our firm is in the midst of an M&A discussion involving one of our portfolio companies. Our investment is five years old, but until now there has never been a good time to exit. However, during the past year, the company's sales have surged by 300 percent. Suddenly it has some big name customers. The company has arisen as a new, tough competitor in the marketplace. And so the board decided to begin exploring its exit opportunities.

The worst time to have to pursue an exit is when the company is not big enough to do an IPO, is not profitable and is running out of working capital. At that point, the board's choices are tough. The board can file for bankruptcy, fire everyone and shut the doors or it can seek an exit hoping to get some of its investment back. Virtually everyone in the VC industry has fought through at least one such situation between 2001 and 2004. In these situations the conundrum for an investor arises from knowing there is some value in the business – for example it may have customers, great intellectual property, a great portfolio of software – but knowing too that the business has failed to produce profits and it will need more working capital to survive to profitability. Often during the 2002-2004 period the prospects of raising capital looked so dim for a company like this that it was impossible to envision how it would build itself up to profitability. Investors have been forced to look for an exit at a loss. Those are the worst times for venture capital. Investors find themselves at the mercy of people who are unlikely to be sympathetic. In these circumstances investors hate to have to sell a good company or (worse still) its remaining assets. But sometimes there is no prudent alternative.

Evaluating an Exit

There are two traditional forms of exit – a sale for cash or an M&A deal. You can divide the M&A deals into two types. The first is one where the acquirer offers a freely tradable public security in exchange for the equity of the acquiree. In these cases investors can evaluate the offer as if it were cash. One can easily evaluate the potential cost or risk in the public security, which is usually publicly available information and the risk is often not great. Investors can view this first type of M&A exit just as they would a cash exit.

The second type of M&A exit is one where the acquirer offers to exchange its restricted securities for the securities of the acquiree. The stock offered may be privately held or restricted in some other way. In these cases the investors will have to wait to sell it or may be unable to sell it for the foreseeable future. Evaluation is difficult and valuation discounts should be applied.

In situations where the acquiree is being offered another private security that investors cannot convert to cash, they must look for a strong security. They must have confidence that the combined companies will have a greater chance of survival and perhaps a better balance sheet. If plans call for the combined company to soon be publicly traded, investors will want to have confidence that it will be priced profitably.

Valuation

Invariably, valuations are driven by reviewing comparable transactions. In an IPO, this process is easy. Everyone can look at publicly traded stocks in the same or similar businesses and consider their price as a multiple of revenues, as a multiple of sales and similar metrics. In the case of private transactions, VCs have a number of sources both in the venture capital industry and on Wall Street that track both private and public M&A transactions. Here too, analysts will compare the price that was paid in comparable deals and correlate it as a multiple of revenues, sales, or other empirical measures.

Occasionally there are more subjective factors that come into play. In the late '90s, we saw people paying for perceived value. For example, consider a company that had no revenues, but had a team of 50 engineers, 20 of whom had PhDs, its product was well along in development, and it had filed a number of promising patent applications. In the late 90s acquirers were inclined to ascribe large values to these intangibles. In 1999, we sold a company where one of the metrics we negotiated over was how much the acquirer should be willing to pay per senior engineer -- because engineering talent was in short supply. The going rate for a brief period then was $500,000 per engineer.

We are unlikely to see such irrationality again but it does illustrate some of the subjective factors that enter into some negotiations. In more prudent markets a valuation negotiation will likely focus primarily on financial multiples. Only after financial performance has been used to create a general range of value will the acquirer or the acquiree take into account subjective factors, such as the portfolio of patents, the intellectual property and the engineering or management talent being acquired. Those subjective factors may then move the price around within that range of multiples. For example, an average multiple of revenues for a given type of business might be 10, but an acquirer may be willing to pay 12 times revenue in order to get a special engineering team or a unique patent portfolio.

Finding a Good Buyer

Defining a good buyer, in other than pure monetary terms, depends on what type of transaction is contemplated. Obviously in the case of a sale for cash, the best buyer is the one who is willing to pay the highest price. By contrast, in an M&A transaction where the sellers will end up with a restricted or a private security, the best buyer is likely to be the one with the stock that the sellers think will have the greatest potential future

THE ROLE OF THE VENTURE CAPITALIST

value. This requires subjective evaluation. A board trying to decide between two potential acquirers, may choose the one offering a pro forma price tag which is lower than another, if the former has better long-term prospects. The seller's board will focus not on current sticker price but on prospective value at the time they will get liquidity out of the transaction. Long-term value should be higher for the acquirer whose management and market prospects are better.

If a company can't find a buyer, there are three options. If it is profitable, the investors can simply wait. If it is not profitable, they then have two choices. They can either invest more capital to get the business to profitability or they can declare bankruptcy and sell the assets for whatever they can salvage.

Completing the Exit Event

An exit transaction will be managed by the board, management, lawyers and (often) investment bankers. But once a transaction closes, everything from that point on is handled by accountants and the CFO. The order and direction of everything that follows the closing should be found in writing. In fact much of it has probably been in writing for years. Each time that a VC made an investment in the company or a creditor loaned money to the company, the transactions will have been documented. These documents spell out the ownership and priority of distribution. These documents dictate behavior for the accountants and the CFO when closing an exit transaction. In most cases the CFO merely fills in the blanks. At the very end of the chain of the distributions will come the venture capitalists' share of the profits and then the ownership of the common shareholders.

If the purchase price happens to be below the value of the original investments in the company, again the documents should spell out what happens. Every deal is different but as a general rule of thumb, the last owner in line for distributions will always be the common stockholders. In a money losing exit, employees who hold options to buy common stock and anyone else who got common instead of preferred stock usually ends up with the short end of the stick, trailing behind those who risked cash.

How Bankruptcy Occurs

Bankruptcy is a choice made by management and the board. We can generalize by saying there are two options: a "Chapter 7" or a "Chapter 11" bankruptcy.

A Chapter 7 bankruptcy is, in layman's terms, when the company effectively declares failure. It asks the court to oversee a process by which it liquidates all its assets and distributes the proceeds to its creditors. In these situations, the creditors sometimes get as little as pennies on every dollar they are owed. There is no plan for a surviving business. The investors can lose everything they have invested.

The alternative is Chapter 11 bankruptcy. This process is used when management and some investors believe the business can survive. The goal in a Chapter 11 proceeding is to come up with a plan to restructure the business and continue operating. The existing equity owners often end up with little unless they hold preferred securities. Preferred stock may carry liquidation priority over some general creditors and common shareholders and thus allow preferred shareholders to gain some ownership in the surviving business. In some cases the preferred stockholders and the secured creditors end up converting their old investment or debt into ownership of a new or surviving entity. Simultaneously the existing investors or new investors must bring in new capital to help the business restart and survive. There have been a great number of these Chapter 11 restructurings between 2001 and 2004 in the technology sectors of the VC industry.

Best Exit Strategy for VCs

Obviously, the best exit strategy for VCs is the one that is most profitable. Every deal is different. Every venture capital firm's intermediate goal is to make a profit for its limited partners/investors. The essence of the venture capital relationship requires that the investors/limited partners must make a profit before the VC/general partner can make a profit. Accordingly, VCs are motivated to create a high IRR, or internal rate of return, from each investment. An internal rate of return is not necessarily what the man in the street would call a high rate of return. For example, if a venture firm doubles the money from an investment, superficially that may sound like a good deal. But, if it has taken seven years to do it, the investment has produced a compounded internal rate of return of barely 10 percent. Such a return may be viewed as a bad deal for a VC and his investors who went into business together hoping to make a 20 percent IRR. On the other hand, if a VC could double its investor's money and get in and out of an investment in twelve months (which would be unusual) then the VC has produced a 100 percent IRR – well in excess of everyone's goals.

In short, everyone involved will look at how long a VC has held an investment and consider the IRR created by an exit. They will compare the IRR with that which might result from a later exit. For example, a VC might get a 50 percent higher price for a company if it waited three years, but waiting may actually lower the rate of return. Timing decisions will be driven by whether waiting might create a higher absolute return but a lower compounded return and by consideration of the risk of waiting for higher returns.

Best Piece of Advice

As with any investment, in any field, a successful investor must be alert for when the time is right to sell. And, it helps to put an experienced person in charge of the process. A VC will rarely let CEOs or engineers or sales and marketing people manage the exit process. Nor should the board let an inexperienced VC or, say, a family investor who happens to be on the board, run the process. Good, experienced professional advisors can be worth far more than they cost.

The best advice of all: if you are offered a profit, take it. Too often investors make the mistake of holding out for too high a price. Believe the old Wall Street adage that there is no such thing as a bad profit.

Jim Murray is the Founder and Managing Director of Court Square Ventures, a venture capital firm specializing in telecommunications and information technology investments, and a founder and former Chairman of Columbia Capital, a venture capital firm that now manages $1.4 billion in private equity. He has been a principal in firms specializing in investment banking and venture capital since 1982.

He is a former Director of Saville Systems Inc. (now merged with ADC Corp.) (NASDAQ "ADCT"). He is Founder/Director of Merrick Tower Corporation, Labrador Communications, LLC and Community Wireless Structures LLC. He is also a Director of Mintera Corp., The NeuroVenture Fund and The Mustique Company, inter alia.

He serves on the executive committee and is Vice Chairman of the Virginia Business Higher Education Council and is past Chairman of the Albemarle County Industrial Development Authority. He has been guest lecturer at the Harvard Business School, the Darden Graduate Business School and the McIntyre School of Commerce at the University of

Virginia. He serves on the North American Board of the Smurfit Graduate Business School, University College, Dublin, Ireland.

Formerly, he was on the board of Advanced Radio Telecom (NASDAQ "ARTT"), Columbia Spectrum Management; President of North Coast Cellular; a Director of Torrent Networking Technologies Corp., Sterling Cellular Systems of New York, and Celutel Inc.; and a Partner in law firm of Richmond & Fishburne, Charlottesville, Virginia.

He received his BA degree from the University of Virginia, his JD from the Marshall-Wythe School of Law at The College of William & Mary and an honorary Doctor of Laws from The College of William & Mary. From 1991-1996, by appointment of the Governor of Virginia, Mr. Murray served on the Board of Visitors of The College of William & Mary and was elected Rector (Chairman) of that Board.

Exit Strategies: Making the Best Decisions

Thomas J. Fogarty, MD
Partner
Three Arch Partners

Looking for an Exit

There are basically two different ways to exit an investment: one is an IPO, the other is an acquisition. Additionally, there are some instances when you can use an IPO to implement the acquisition. If the economic environment is right, you could use an IPO to accrue additional cash so that you can ramp up sales and profitability, which will make your offering more attractive to a potential buyer.

From a venture standpoint, limited partners expect a return on their investment. This can take the form of cash or stock in the acquiring company or a distribution of stock from the IPO. Essentially, the investors in the venture community, the limited partners, and the general partners have to provide a return on the capital they have used.

In the startup community, the best time to pursue an exit strategy is when the value of your company is highest. At times, this involves making a judgment call; whether you should do an IPO or be acquired is not always a clear-cut decision. You need to look at the history of the company and the product, and then identify the point of optimal value.

The worst time to exit is when you are in need of money; at this point, your value has already decreased. A growing market offers the best conditions for selling. For example, there was a time when one of the primary objectives in the medical marketplace was to make people live longer. Now, however, there is a strong emphasis on living better as well. If your product or technology addresses both living longer and living better, then you have addressed a strong market need and optimized your return. Even in a weak economy, if you address what society is asking for it will be a good time to exit.

Roles of VC, CEO, CFO

VC

A venture capitalist is usually part of the company board, and the decision about when to exit is customarily made by the board. The responsibilities of a venture player differ from those of management. For example, the limited partners in a venture firm expect a return on their capital. If a venture firm does not have much experience in exits, they may be more anxious to exit at a lower value just to obtain a return. Management however, might think they can optimize the value with an additional year of operations, which requires additional money. This funding usually comes from the venture community. The needs of the company's management and venture investor are not always in sync.

CEO

When pursuing an exit strategy, the role of the CEO is absolutely critical. The CEO tells the company's story, presents the "road show," and talks to the people who would buy the stock in the initial public offering. A CEO needs to have great credibility; he or she must be able to demonstrate the company's value.

The CEO can contribute significantly to the success of initial public offerings, and having credible, well-known venture investors is also helpful. It's important to have a CEO who has been part of the process and who has brought the company to a point where people see clearly that it works. A CEO needs to demonstrate that he or she has managed the process well and worked with the board and the venture investors to optimize the company's value.

CFO

The CFO also plays a critical role during an IPO. The CFO's role is to tell the company's financial story extremely well and to demonstrate clearly how the company's margins will improve once scalability is achieved in manufacturing, sales, and distribution.

When an IPO is the Right Exit Strategy

The process of exiting by an IPO is fairly simple; in the current environment, there are certain straightforward requirements to do an IPO. One is that you have to be at the break-even or early stages of profitability. You also must have a preamble that demonstrates a ramp that is progressively and consistently increasing.

Following an interview process, your board engages a banker that it believes will be most effective. The banker then works with your company to create a book that outlines what the company is doing and why; this is basically the sales pitch. You then approach an institutional investor who may be interested in your initial public offering.

Bankers use various means to evaluate a company. They look at the value of companies in the same field. They look at a list of companies to see what their stock prices and market caps are, and they compare those factors to what you have to offer in that same space. They look at how much market share you are taking away from some of these companies and whether you are able to accomplish that consistently.

Determining what percentage of the company to sell to the public is a judgment call. Your goal is to give as little away as possible. When you do a public offering, your bankers determine a range within which they think they can sell the company. In a weakened economy, you may end up selling more of the company than you would like.

Negotiations are delicate. The bankers inform the board as to what they think they can get per share on exit, then the board either accepts or rejects the amount. Part of a banker's challenge is dealing with expectations that are too high and that can sour potential investors. It doesn't help the company or the board if the banker is told to offer a range of 15 to 20 when the right range is 13 to 15. In that case, the banker should advise the board that doing so would be a waste of everyone's time.

Best Type of Exit Strategy for a VC

A VC has several options when it comes to an exit strategy: an IPO, an acquisition, or an IPO followed by an acquisition. A VC can leave with either cash or stock; in the current economic environment there is very little cash. Whatever money a company receives goes to the operational plan of the company, and little of the money goes to management.

An IPO brings cash to the company so that it can implement its plans and, hopefully, be successful. If you are being acquired by a company, some of your management may or may not go with the acquiring company. Being acquired usually spells the end of the story for the VCs, except when the acquiring company does not want much stock traded within a certain timeframe. The specific scenario depends on the environment and what you negotiate.

You have to decide which is best for your company – an IPO or being acquired. Right now, the IPO market is relatively non-existent so an IPO is not a sound decision unless your ramp rate is truly compelling. In that case, your monthly revenues would have to be increasing by a highly significant percentage, and you would be at a threshold where achieving profitability will occur in a predictable timeframe.

The valuations on an initial public offering are much lower now, which means you could end up giving more of the company away for less money. Given that situation, being acquired by a large company that needs your technology might produce greater value for you.

Process of Exiting with an Acquisition

When pursuing a buyer, you need to look at companies already in the marketplace or companies that should be in that marketplace but aren't. That knowledge is gained through experience and by knowing the players.

In some situations a major company is aware of your product and will approach you to let you know they are interested and to establish a relationship. The relationship could start as a sales distribution relationship with a timeline leading to an acquisition. At the opposite extreme, a major company may identify a technology you have that they have an interest in and begin talking about acquisition right away.

The acquisition process usually comes about from negotiations that occur between the two companies; however, investment bankers are part of the process. Because there has been a decline in the number of IPOs, investment bankers are working with large companies and the venture capital community and dealing with financial levels well below where they used to be when the economy was strong. Many bankers would not look at a deal unless a company was raising a minimum of $50 million to $100 million. With the decline in the IPO market, bankers are now acting as intermediaries in establishing something as simple as a sales distribution agreement. In these cases, they hope that the agreement will lead to an acquisition in which they will be the agent.

If a company can't find a buyer and needs cash to survive, there aren't many options from which to choose. You can continue to fund the company from the venture community and sell it at a loss or you can declare bankruptcy. With bankruptcy, you liquidate your assets in the hope that you can pay off your debts to the investors.

Completing an Exit Event: Common vs. Preferred Stock

A startup company has common stock and preferred stock. In the exit, the preferred stock converts to the common. Depending on the structure of the deal, preferred stock usually gets all the money before the common gets any. The common shareholders consist of the management and the founders. The preferred shareholders are the individuals who put in hard cash at a value higher than the common price. It makes sense, then, that the preferred get their money first. On exit, the preferred is first and the common is second.

If the purchase price is below the original value, the common stock takes the hit since those shareholders didn't put any money in or if they did, it was at a very low price. Usually the differential between preferred and common stock at the outset of funding is 10 to 1; the common is usually one-tenth of the price of the preferred.

Lockup is the period after the IPO during which original money is legally prohibited from selling any shares of company stock. Lockup can last anywhere from three months to two years. Unless other arrangements are made with original investors, the lockup usually applies to the venture community and the company management. The length of the lockup depends on what is negotiated within the framework of the IPO.

Factors You Can and Can't Control in an Exit

In an exit, the one factor you can control is offering a product that is needed, easy to use, and cost effective. Your time is best spent optimizing your product offering; the exit becomes the secondary issue. You shouldn't work to exit – you should work to optimize products. Individuals in the company should allocate their time to making the best possible product instead of worrying about how they will exit.

Realistically, the timeline for exiting a position after making an investment is three to ten years. The economic environment is the most important factor in timing an exit. A company's need for your technology is the second most important factor.

A third factor is when a large company wants to establish a presence in a given market and they may become very aggressive about early acquisitions. The greater the need in the marketplace for a technology, the more attractive it becomes for acquisition. The small startups excel at developing products that address a need in the marketplace. Often, however, they cannot afford to spend a great deal of money on the infrastructure for sales and distribution. On the other hand, large companies usually have money available for that type of infrastructure. They can get a developed technology to the marketplace much more quickly than a startup can.

When considering exit strategies, one of the factors that can't be controlled is the general economic environment. When evaluations of publicly held stocks are either holding steady or going down, companies aren't interested in making significant investments. As the dividends go down in a slow economic environment, stock value goes down. To put it simply, when the economic climate is poor, people hang on to cash.

If you are looking at acquisitions, you cannot control senior management, which may change rather frequently. The president of a major corporation that decides it wants to be in a certain market may move on to another position; the person who replaces him or her may have a totally different perspective and a different plan for the company.

Successful Exit Strategies

Successful exit strategies come about from three things: emphasizing the value of the product, emphasizing the value of the team, and being able to tell the company story in an understandable manner that reflects financial reality.

One of the most frequent mistakes entrepreneurs make when trying to pursue an exit strategy is not listening to people who have experience and expertise. It's important for entrepreneurs and CEOs to avoid confusing knowledge with wisdom. Far too often people accumulate vast amounts of knowledge but fail to develop wisdom. In regard to exit strategies, the combination of both knowledge and wisdom is what ultimately gets you to a successful endpoint.

Dr. Thomas Fogarty is an internationally recognized cardiovascular surgeon, inventor, and entrepreneur. He has founded or co-founded over 30 companies in the medical device or services field, many based on devices designed and developed at Fogarty Research. He also actively participates as co-founder and Senior Partner in the venture capital firm of Three Arch Partners.

Making Strategic Company Investments

Matthew Insley Growney
Co-Founder & Managing Director
Motorola Ventures

Developing an Exit Strategy

From the time you research and source a possible investment opportunity, the strategy is to always find a tangible customer base. For instance, when investing in technology, you might get a Motorola or an Intel or Microsoft to actually be part of the technology's development. These large corporations can then take some ownership of that technology and design it into their own products. Fostering that early partnership can create a good acquisition candidate scenario. Down the road, if a larger company has been working with a start-up for two or three years on multiple product families or multiple technology generations, it is usually a pretty good bet that they will look at acquiring the company so that they can fully exploit the technology.

Cisco has been a proponent of that, as has Motorola. Motorola, Inc. has acquired two of Motorola Ventures' portfolio companies in the past eighteen months. The reason is that Motorola product groups were involved with the startup companies' technology at the time that Motorola Ventures made the investments. Both Motorola product groups and the Motorola Ventures portfolio companies collaborated and co-developed numerous technology applications and understood what it could do for its own products. It was an eventuality that Motorola would consider buying the companies outright. That is one of the strategies.

When we make investments in companies, we look at what is truly the customer base or the customer target. This important understanding is coupled with a finite view of an emerging market or larger existing market opportunity. Within that targeted customer base, a portfolio company doesn't just sell them a product, but actually shares with them white papers and technical specifications, and discusses what custom solutions they could use. Both a possible large customer and startup company begin a series of good faith discussions on technology exploration and eventually a project agreement. We (as startup companies) try to attract these big customers early on so that in three or four years, they find that they can't live without the technology.

Timeline for Exiting a Position

These days we are generally looking to exit an investment within three to four years. In three or four years, everything reinvents itself in the communications and technology industries. A factor that might change the timeline of an exit would be a delay in some kind of industry standards body. If we are making investments in technologies that are not yet making it into an accepted standard, we are not going to exit them. Instead, we will try to establish the portfolio company as an industry standard or standards compliant so that we can commercialize the technology. You would hate to make an investment in a company that never becomes a standard -- the beta vs. VHS problem. That is one thing that could really hold up our timeline. Another is technology. There may be an underestimation of the ability to integrate certain technologies into products. In those cases, we are not going to give up just because the timeline is not met.

The competitiveness of the market segment could also alter the timeline. If all of a sudden we notice after a year of making an investment that there are five or six other competitors that have evolved, we are going to try to make sure we have the best solution so that we can go after as much market share as possible. That may mean being invested longer than three years and maybe spending an extra year on marketing so that we can move from 10 percent market share to 30 percent, 40 percent or 50 percent market share.

Exiting an Investment

Cutting your losses, not throwing bad money after good, is an obvious way to mitigate any future risk. Being able to do that is certainly a challenge for venture capital firms because the companies were initially very promising. VCs can get into a vicious circle where they will bridge the company more money and then a little more money because they keep thinking that it will only take a little bit more time and money to turn the company around. The reality is that it never gets turned around. Two or three years later, they are out millions of dollars beyond their initial investment and the company has gone bankrupt.

One of the ways that we try to avoid this is to attempt to understand what the management is capable of doing once we have noticed that the company is not performing very well. Are they able to turn this around? Is short-term funding going to help solve the problem? Are there tangible customers for the company's technology today? We go through this critical analysis with the board of directors and the management team. If they cannot deliver the product or they have consistently been unable to do what they said they would do, we look for an exit. The best way to exit is to either sell our shares back to the company at some sort of discount or call a convertible note if we have bridged the company debt financing and simply demand payment or work out some sort of settlement. These are the sorts of ugly ways that we try to prevent ourselves from getting into the vicious cycle of continuing to throw money into something that is fundamentally broken.

A lot of the decision is determined by talking to the customers. We try to understand whether or not the company is actually communicating to the right people and if they are communicating a clear message to potential customers. If after a month, a potential customer doesn't understand why they need the product, obviously the startup company is not communicating their technology solution well enough, which may mean they have broken marketing and sales. We try to go to the outside to find out what is wrong inside. That also means going back to MIT or the university scientist level and breaking down the technology. Once we have that perspective, we are then quickly able to make a decision about whether we are going to stick around or cut our losses and move on.

We have been fortunate enough to build customers and revenue streams to develop companies that are attractive for third party acquisitions. We've been able to have our companies really show their value from a sales perspective so that they actually have customers willing to buy the technology. We may stop technology development just so we can focus on the sales and marketing aspects of these companies. By doing that, we were able to make some good multiples when we sold several of our companies to third party acquirers.

We really don't comment on the IPO market because there have not been any that have gone public. Everything has been mostly private trade sale because institutional investors are no longer willing to take risks on 100-person companies with inexperienced boards. That was a phenomenon of the late 1990s. Now institutional investors want to see much longer track records and much more positive growth from these 100-150 person start-ups before they are willing to put their firm behind them. That is one reason.

The other reason is that in a depressed economy, there are a lot of companies that find it easier to just buy little private companies than to buy a company that has gone public and raised a bunch of cash. A lot of these younger companies don't need to aspire to an IPO. They simply can aspire to be bought at a very healthy decent multiple from larger companies hungry to build product lines.

When we exit by selling, we are at the table in either a board director capacity or as an observer. We are also very intimately involved with the management team at the company. We have to understand what the incentives are for selling the company and what we are hoping to accomplish from a financial perspective, as well as what this means for the technology. We go through those scenarios with the management and the board and then we ask for a formal offer sheet. These are discussed at the board level and the management level and then we usually put together either a merger acquisition committee at the board or we appoint an investment banker from the outside to help interface with the potential acquirer or acquirers. If there is no clause stating otherwise, then you are able to start a bidding process. That usually takes place over the course of a month or two. Once you determine what the tangible offers are, you begin to negotiate the details. At that point it doesn't take long to execute the transaction.

Best Time to Pursue an Exit Strategy

One key time to pursue an exit strategy is the distress asset, which is when a company has been unable to raise more money and will probably run out of cash within the next 90 days. We then look for a way to sell the team as a whole so the employees can stay together with the competency that they have developed. They go with the technology. That is usually an asset sale of some sort, generally at 10-40 cents on the dollar.

The other good time is when a company has really started to pick up speed. It has multiple customers and is operating at a fairly good positive cash flow, but perhaps its margins are not very big because it cannot get to the next big step of building out. At that point, it's a good time to test the merger and acquisition market. In doing that, you will find some of your biggest customers and see how seriously they are committed to the development of your technology and your company and propose to them that they buy the company. If they buy the company, you can leverage their resources to go after bigger markets.

A company in that situation probably has 40-60 employees, the technology has been pretty well tested and it has customers. It just can't get to that next hurdle without someone to help it leverage resources or allocate resources to it as a new subsidiary. We have done that several times as well. We have bought companies that were at the stage where they had the potential for mass-market appeal but they really needed Motorola to buy them and allow them to leverage our distribution channels.

Best Exit Strategy for Management

The best exit strategy for management varies a great deal based on whether the management team is still made up of the founders or whether or not they are going to go with a potential acquirer. Is it an asset purchase or a company purchase? Those factors really affect management's view of what is best for them. If they have an employee base of 20 or 30 people who they have been working with for a long time and they have a lot of attachment to the company, they may think it would be best is to be acquired by a huge Fortune 500 company where they could continue to work on the technology that they helped birth. Any management team would be comfortable with that -- insuring the future employment of their employees and still being able to be attached to the technology.

Others may have greed as an incentive. Maybe you have a third-time entrepreneur who didn't do very well the first two times and now has a chance to make a lot of money. They will come down to the highest offer, not necessarily the best offer. There are other management teams that have been brought in who aren't founders and aren't really attached to the company. They were brought in by the board just to fix the company up to sell it. Those guys are not interested in sticking around and are more interested in accomplishing their goal, which is to get an offer on the table to sell the company so they can move on to the next cleanup job.

The Only Exit Strategy for the VC

The only exit strategy for the VC is usually to divest its holdings through a monetization at the highest valuation possible. Greed prevails in the traditional venture capital realm. I have not heard of too many VCs who have turned down an offer to exit their investment because it was "too high." The VC's incentive is to return money to his or her limited partners and that is it. Motorola Ventures and other investment groups have very different opinions. We have made investments in companies because we believe they will become customers or partners of Motorola. I need to make sure that the relationships with companies we sell to the outside world remain intact because there is a very good chance we will continue to work together. We would hate to see those management people be laid off or disappear. That intellectual capital is very valuable to us. We want to ensure that it sticks around. My goal is not to lose money, of course, but to be cash flow even and make sure the employees in startup companies that we sell are going to be around to advocate Motorola as a good investment partner.

The Role of a VC

When selling a company, the VC has legal duties and corporate duties. The legal duties are based around the ability to be objective and act as a champion of the company to make sure there are no transactions that are done in bad faith or that could be damaging to shareholders. The VC has a duty of loyalty and a duty of care to make sure that a potential acquisition is in the best interest of the shareholders. That may be different from the VC's own interests because he may not be an investor in the company if he is an independent or outside director. He needs to put his own personal feelings aside and understand what an offer means to the whole shareholder base. If he does not represent an objective, good faith point of view, he could certainly have legal action brought by shareholders or other investors.

There are also other responsibilities a VC needs to practice when looking at acquisitions. From an efficiency standpoint, we need to make sure that we are looking at these offers in a timely fashion and not dragging out the process or being unresponsive to a potential acquirer. It is in everyone's best interest, including the company's, to be efficient with the review because you can't leave employees on edge wondering whether or not they will get sold.

A board director or VC should be also running an analysis on what this offer really means in good faith. What is the offer we are getting? Is this really the best offer? Is it determined by just the money or by who is buying us? What have other companies gone through in comparable situations? To me, there is a level of diligence that a board director or VC should have when he is aiding and facilitating one of his companies through the acquisition process. In the end, all parties involved should have an amicable relationship intact and certainly a professional one.

Generally, there is a lead person, usually a VC, responsible for interfacing with the acquirer. It is really difficult to have the whole board work directly with the acquirer on setting terms and negotiating because there are just too many chefs in the kitchen. Some companies handle everything through investment banks so they don't get involved in communicating with the acquirer at all.

The Role of Management

The CEO clearly needs to represent his employees' best interests. He also needs to be cognizant of the technology that has been developed by the company. Along with intellectual capital, that is their core asset. How does an acquisition affect those assets? That is the role the CEO really needs to play when a company is involved in an acquisition. They should also be contributing to the acquisition analysis or participating on a merger or acquisition committee to make sure they are communicating their employees' concerns to the board and to the potential acquirer.

Employees should certainly always feel like they are involved and have an open channel of communication with their board or senior management during an acquisition analysis. A lot of companies are sold at distressed prices and things don't go down very smoothly, so a lot of employees leave. You then lose the intellectual value they had as an employee and they may go to your competitor. Employees should be encouraged to voice their concerns to the CEO or board.

Deciding When to Sell the Company

Usually the decision to sell the company comes about by a triumvirate agreement between investors, management and the acquirer. Those three groups are required to constructively analyze an exit. Unless there are but a few investors owning a significant amount of shares, all three groups are typically involved in an active discussion over who and when to sell the company. There really isn't one party that can force a sale more than the next because each has a very compelling leverage piece at a certain point.

In good cases, all three are very actively involved in the negotiation and the agreement, they give the handshake, sign a term sheet and then the acquisition is done. However, there are cases when the investor base ends up owning such a significant part of the company that they can eliminate the management vote in a company's sale. That becomes a dangerous model, because management that does not feel like they are involved could quit, hijack the offer or do a whole host of other things that would be detrimental to all three parties.

Evaluating a Company

When evaluating a company, some of it is economics, such as revenue, multiples of revenue and discounted cash flow models on the company's performance. There are also other metrics such as what comparable companies were sold at and the multiples they were sold at during different times of their growth stages. People run a whole host of PE multiples and market cap analysis. There is also the amount of money the company has received. For instance, if we know we are not going to make any money, we at least want to make back what we have put in. Many times they will use valuation models based on how much money the company has been financed. There are other things like the market analysis. You start to go through numbers and extensive analysis on market size. There are a whole slew of these financial models, and certainly financial analysis and modeling is done to come up with a number, but at the end of the day there is also an element of what someone will pay for it.

There are some macro market conditions that do affect valuation, but ultimately it is about longer-term growth. I don't know very many companies that are buying startup companies because they have an immediate gap and must generate revenue starting tomorrow. For the most part, market conditions may play a casual part in determining evaluation but the primary factor that sets the price is what will be paid for the company today, not an outside variable.

Pursuing a Good Buyer

Buyers are looking for companies that have a gap in a growth area that they think they can develop. You need to get as much communication to these potential acquirers as possible to sell them on why you think you have the solution for a gap. We have seen this on several occasions. It doesn't make sense to try to sell your company to a company that has no cash, doesn't see the longer-term vision or doesn't appreciate your technology.

From an acquisition perspective, usually if you find two very synergistic types of companies, the two boards will try to merge the company to create one stronger company. It has happened on several occasions that our company shared the same pain points as another company, and both boards felt the two companies should be pulled together to save resources. For us, that is usually a good solution to give the company new life.

Completing an Exit

Upon completion of an exit event, the payment is usually through preferences. Most venture capital deals set up liquidation preferences in the event that the company is sold. Essentially those who participated in the most recent amount of risk deserve to be paid the most first. They are paid at the highest risk amount or risk profile. You pay over a period of time so that you don't have to assume the expense all up front. Others are milestones where you will pay a flat price of $15 million, but should the company actually do very, very well over the next six months, you will pay $17 million. There are different ways to structure the payouts.

Most Frequent Mistakes of Entrepreneurs

One of the most frequent mistakes entrepreneurs make when trying to pursue an exit strategy is not communicating with the board and trying to get the deal done themselves. Sometimes this is done because the CEO is desperate or because he thinks he has a better contact base, but it is really a damaging way to put your company up for sale. The same thing happens with VCs who are investors. Investors who do not communicate and instead call up their network or chat casually with people about acquisitions are also damaging. All of a sudden the word on the Street is that your company is for sale, but nothing has been said about it officially so everyone thinks you are in trouble. You have to put up a unified front as a board and as a management team and to do that, you can't have these offline communications.

Best Piece of Advice About Exit Strategies

I always tell everyone to be patient and to be diligent about the process. Those two are the most communicated. A lot of CEOs are very eager to take the first offer and get out. There is a whole host of ways that you can go through a process in a very patient manner and really understand the idea behind who is buying you and what they are offering. If a potential acquirer is giving you five days to make a decision to sell what you have worked five years on, that is not a person you want to be in partnership with. You need to really understand what is being offered for your company and what they intend to do with your company so that you don't get into trouble or have to go back and sue the company later for a breach of warranty or covenants that may or may not be in the term sheet.

Golden Rules for Successful Exit Strategies

One of the golden rules for successful exit strategies is to make sure that when you are growing your company, you are doing it with customers in mind. We don't like to make investments in technologies that are scientist proven. We want technologies that are technologist proven. There is a very fundamental difference. Scientists can't sell things. Technologists can.

When you are developing a new company, make sure that you have a customer and a segment in mind because those customers are going to come back. If you develop relationships with them, they will come back to not only help fund your ongoing activities but they will also pay for your product, and many times they will buy the company. You are diversifying your client base as well as the potential number of acquirers who might buy your company down the road. You are also increasing your relationship base and your network base, which may represent in the future different suppliers or channels of distribution. Pay attention to the customer even from the time that you incorporate and you have no customers.

The second golden rule is to make sure you have a sound, professional board of directors and strong corporate governance. I cannot emphasize enough that just because we are not in a public market and just because this isn't NASDAQ, that doesn't mean we are exempt from corporate governance duties. You need to make sure that when you are going into an acquisition that you have a board of directors that can be unified when they are negotiating and operating with a potential offer in best faith and with best efforts. That is crucial. Otherwise you will never get your company sold.

Matthew I. Growney is a co-founder and Managing Director of Motorola Ventures, based in Cambridge, Massachusetts. His role is to actively review, invest, and manage the global minority equity opportunities strategic to Motorola's core and emerging businesses including communications and embedded solutions. Such key areas of investment include interactive television, home networking, personal area networks, energy solutions, and embedded software.

Prior to co-founding Motorola Ventures, Matthew successfully completed three diverse positions as a Commodities Buyer with Motorola's Land Mobile Product Sector, Corporate Development Analyst at Nippon Motorola Limited in Tokyo, Japan, and as the Business Analyst for Motorola's Corporate Strategy-Business Development office. His primary responsibilities included management of unsolicited deal flow, investment tracking, and merger and acquisition analysis. In 1999, Matthew also conducted cyber-law, e-commerce, and domain name legal review on behalf of HSD Ernst & Young- France in Paris, France.

Matthew has studied C++ Programming at Harvard University and International Civil Law at the University of San Jose in Costa Rica. He graduated from Michigan State University and possesses a Juris Doctor degree from the New England School of Law in Boston. Matthew sits on the boards of Xanboo. He also sits on the Board of Advisors for the Global Venture Network in New York City and Shanghai, as well as Capital Venue of Boston. Additionally, Matthew is Vice President of the Corporate Venturing Consortium for MIT's Sloan School EDP program. Outside of Motorola, Matthew is a Board Director for TodoBebe, a young media company serving young families throughout Latin America and involved in various charities serving Boston's homeless. He is also a Founding Advisor of Sigma Capital Partners, a boutique private equity firm in Manhattan.

VC Exits: A European Perspective

Mark Clement

Managing Director
Merlin Biosciences

Factors Affecting the Timeline

The primary business model for exiting mid-stage and early-stage companies is a company that is capable of sustaining value at IPO within the usual three-to-five-year and five-to-seven-year hold times. That would be a question of the companies' ability to mature and then make an initial public offering (IPO), or to achieve a trade sale in a slightly more mature manner.

If the stock markets were to prove more receptive to earlier-stage companies, it would certainly tempt my company, Merlin, to put these companies on the market sooner. Also, if a trade buyer came to us and we could identify an opportunity to achieve an earlier exit perhaps at lower risk, then we would weigh that out.

For Merlin, as a biotechnology investor, these businesses are rarely cash-positive and therefore; they have the need to be refinanced. With each subsequent refinancing, we are at the mercy of the private markets in terms of valuation and the basis under which we are able to participate. The concept of dilution or a deprioritization on things like liquidation preferences means we would not be in as strong a position. Sometimes it is better to do an earlier exit to avoid any potential dilution on subsequent rounds. People need to be aware of these dynamics.

Your exit strategy should be part of your pre-investment appraisal. You need to start with the end in mind. You have to go into these companies with a very clear idea about how they need to look at various stages and what your primary exit objectives are. I would very much start with the end in mind.

In our industry, if you presume that all of your companies will go to IPO, you are being very naïve. I believe our default strategy must be trade sale. An IPO opportunity is a bonus.

Exit by IPO

Traditionally when you do an IPO, you have a listing on a primary market in one of the major exchanges. We place the company's stocks on the public market and try to sell those shares in the aftermarket, usually by means of some sort of bought deal or bargain trade – a block trade.

Other routes would be to have a trade sale to a larger group either for cash or for paper, which could be private or public. If it were public, our hope would be that we would be able to place those shares in the market. If it were private, our ultimate aim would be that the enlarged company would then progress toward some sort of liquidity event either through an IPO or a trade sale. Those are the two primary exit routes we would focus on.

Exit by Trade Sale

The results of a trade sale depend on the nature of the deal, whether it is a cash transaction – very few of them are – or a paper transaction. If it is a paper transaction, it is usually either private paper you are taking in consideration, or public paper. The process of distributing cash to shareholders on a cash sale is quite straightforward.

Once the deal has gone wholly unconditional – that is, you've satisfied various conditions; representations and warranties have been made; due diligence has been undertaken; and contracts have been signed – then the cash would be effectively handed over for distribution to the shareholders.

For a number of cash deals involving technology companies, there is usually some deferred consideration or some sort of retention held back so that the acquiring company can test that things are what they seem to be. There is usually some sort of deferral, traditionally between 10 percent and 25 percent of the cash consideration. A cash deal is relatively straightforward.

For paper transactions, the process can be slightly more complicated for the selling company. If you have to accept paper, you need to make assessments of the company; whereas, if someone is paying you cash you don't have to ask what sort of cash it is. Cash is cash.

For the buying company in a paper deal, you need to look more deeply into the company to which you're giving the cash. You would expect to be doing some due diligence. If it is a public company, that can be limited only to publicly available information. If it were a private company, the due diligence would be fairly extensive. At the end of the day, you need to feel comfortable that the paper you'll get will retain its value in the aftermarket.

If the company is public, you normally are asked to sign what is known as a lock-in arrangement, whereby you would undertake not to sell certain shares in the aftermarket, and that would be dealt with in due course. If you are being bought by a huge company, and you end up with perhaps less than 3 percent or 4 percent of the free float, there is less concern about what we call orderly market undertakings. For a merger of equals or one in which you have a significant percentage, you would be asked to lock in, so you would undertake not to place the shares for a period of usually six to nine months.

IPO Strategies

Valuations in our industry are to some extent governed by people's sentiment. An IPO is the right strategy when, as a venture capitalist, you clearly can achieve a true understanding of the fundamentals of a business, and you can create enough appetite within the public markets to support not just the primary offering, but also the secondary market, where you think you can trade your stock out. If your primary aim for these cash-negative companies is to raise cash to develop the business and then to support the business and create an opportunity for you to sell your shares, it has to be done when the markets understand what is going on. Over the last three years, the markets simply have not been open, so you haven't had a choice. Sentiment is a major driver.

Certain companies are not likely to offer the sort of broader range of attractions to capital investors; they don't offer capacity for significant capital growth. They may be a little more pedestrian in what they want to achieve. For those companies that fulfill a particular requirement and address a particular issue but are not likely to provide broader business platforms, you could argue that trade sale is a more realistic option than an IPO, so some things are better suited for trade sale than IPO.

Obviously, from a timing point of view, if you want to do a quick flip – that is, get into an early-stage situation and develop it enough through proof of principle – it may not have the substance and the maturity to merit a presence on a public market, but it may be an ideal quick trade sale. Again, you can trade a little where the balance of the company is in its development and also where the interest is.

How Much to Sell and at What Value?

How much to sell to the public is usually determined by the sponsors – the investment banks responsible for that. They usually want to insure at a minimum liquidity of 25 percent of the company. The focus is primarily on raising new money for the company, not on satisfying exiting venture capitalists. I would say, on average, between 25 percent and 33 percent of the company is usually made available at IPO for new money, but that's decided by the banks.

Determining the right valuation is more of an art than a science. I think it is becoming more of a science as the sector matures, but in our area, you can't do multiples of historic or prospective earnings because usually there aren't any. You have to be able to anticipate the future state of the company in terms of its potential products, risk-adjust the positioning of those products on the market, and anticipate their success in their market in terms of the amount of money they can make.

There is a forecasting system, which is a risk-adjusted net present value with heavy discounts. This makes the net present value of the future pipeline heavily subjective. You can compare the company with one at a similar stage or in a similar area and take references as to whether it is better or worse. There are a number of yardsticks in terms of the composites that people put together to try to ascribe values to certain parts of the asset base or the deals that have been done. The fundamental analyses have largely been discounted. It is now more a question of looking at comparables and predicting how the company is likely to perform in the aftermarket.

The aim is to ensure that there are some good prospects of capital growth for the people who come in at the IPO. If you are pricing the company so that it goes to a big discount in the aftermarket, then you have overpriced it, and institutions don't like that.

The Different Players

There is no generic role a venture capitalist plays because there are different sorts of venture capitalists. There are followers and leaders.

The leaders tend to have industry background, with a range of business experiences themselves. Some of them may well have had their own businesses. They are frequently mentors and hands-on investors.

This group can play a pivotal role in achieving an IPO. For example, they are able to judge the correct profile, the right timing in balancing between maturing the company and not using up too much cash, the positioning of the company in terms of the key messages, the communication process, and the selection of an IPO sponsor. They will be heavily involved in pricing discussions and the positioning. This venture capitalist will play a pivotal role in determining how the whole process will work. We find ourselves being quite instrumental in making the process work.

The followers play a more passive role. They will certainly be involved in a more legalistic sense because their approval is needed at various stages. But they don't actually get involved in the process.

The CEO and the CFO are the primary players. The CEO is very much the exponent. He or she must talk in a very authoritative and convincing manner about the business, the strategy, the business model, the value drivers, the dynamic. Everything that goes to the core of the proposal and the offering will be run by his or her voice. From a communication point of view, the CEO is the lead player.

The CFO will have a larger role in managing the internal process – a highly mechanistic approach that requires heavy financial, legal, and administrative input. The CFOs traditionally are responsible for making the process work, whereas the CEO sells the process and makes and drives the actual offering in the marketplace. Together, the CEO and CFO are often the double act on which many people will base their investment.

Steps to Value the Company

Valuation in our industry is a function of many elements:

- Your products and their stage of development
- The probability that they'll reach market
- Risk factors
- The market size of those products, once they reach market
- Your likely profit on sales

The value of your intellectual property and your core competence in management – your ability to make things happen – are intangible. You have to profile the business and anticipate where the business will develop. You must be able to assess costs to develop the business, work out the markets you will be in, and develop models. You need to judge the inherent value, and then do comparative analyses with other groups in that area. You'll arrive at a hybrid approach to valuating the company. These steps need to be done rigorously and objectively.

When selling the company, you then need to get on board experienced advisors who have broad transactional skills in identifying partners, valuating businesses, and supporting the closing and negotiation completion process.

Handling Negotiations in a Trade Sale/Purchase

Negotiations must be done with integrity and professionalism. You need to establish a basis for dialog, a framework for negotiating. You need to be able to consistently apply a basis valuation that is common to both companies, and both must understand the framework so that when differences arise, you have ways to discuss them and create resolutions.

The process of negotiation needs to be led by a combination of principals, usually the CEO, CFO, or business development director and advisors. Throughout the process, there should be a sense of cooperation and a fairly strong sense of commercial reality. In communicating with the other board members, a committee of shareholders usually acts with the CEO negotiating teams to update, at various stages, the zone of comfort and the executives' scope of authority. The common dialog among the shareholders, the board, and the negotiating team promotes their confidence in knowing they can deliver that which they have negotiated.

Pursuing a Good Strategic Buyer

A good strategic buyer needs to have an existing presence within a market of choice and a solid understanding about what it takes to be successful within a particular sector. They also need a strong sense of commitment regarding the resources they are prepared to allocate to the market, to the product you are selling them, and to the business. It's also important for the buyer to be realistic about what needs to be achieved.

Certainly thorough domain knowledge, deep financial commitment, and clearly available resources are critical to identifying a good buyer. A credible strategy with a realistic timeline for developing the markets and a willingness to translate their plans into actions are important elements of the process that show they are wedded to the opportunity.

If your company can't find a buyer, you should continue to develop it until it is attractive. Your inability to find a buyer now doesn't mean you can't find a buyer tomorrow; the problem may be only the need to mature what you have. It may be a question of searching more broadly; there could be buyers in the market that you haven't found. You have to make your own "luck": You must create opportunities to make buyers aware of you and attract them to you.

Walking Away from a Company

Our style as a group is to be extremely methodical and hands-on about what we get into. If something doesn't work, the reason is usually that the science is flawed, management is not good, or the market is suspect.

If the science is fundamentally flawed, there is not a lot we can do to change that, so we work to conserve the cash. That is rule number one. Rule number two: If there is a management problem, we replace the management, and with the cash we conserved and the new management, we reengineer the company. We have to be unafraid to take these measures.

A number of things have to happen before you decide to walk away from a company. Usually walking away is the last resort. It most often means we failed in our attempts to salvage the company. Generally, VCs can do great work if they have the right control mechanisms and if they can change management and conserve the cash. When VCs can't influence management or control the cash, the ride will be steep and rocky.

Completion of an Exit Event

When you finance a private company, each successive round of financing will have a priority over the prior class or classes. The more recent the money is, usually the higher its priority. It will have certain benefits over other classes of shares. As you put more money in, because your money means the difference between the company's existing or not, in the event of a trade sale, you would get your money back before others; you are ahead in the queue.

The first thing you do when you have an exit is to work out your preference – that is, your standing in the actual queue, your priority. Companies usually are not sold; they are bought. If you want to persuade the buyer, you have to leave something on the table for management. Even though they may not be an institutional shareholder, you have to offer some incentive, a liquidation preference. It will usually be an element that is made safe for the people who will make the sale happen.

You get management first. Then you get the more recent shareholders out, and then you work down the chain.

If the purchase price is below the original value, the priority people will end up getting their money, but the others will get nothing. Ultimately the investors at the back of the queue will go hungry.

Most Frequent Mistakes in Pursuing an Exit

The most frequent mistake entrepreneurs make when trying to pursue an exit is to be greedy and ask for too much. They make their own continued involvement with the company a precondition of the company going forward. They will put their own egos and their own personal agendas ahead of the company's best interest.

Many investors truly do not understand that the process of exiting is complex. It is quite a demanding issue requiring a phenomenal level of commitment and focus. This kind of investing is not something you can do on a part-time basis. The amount of time and energy involved is enormous. Too many people underestimate this requirement.

In the European context, the best piece of advice I could give is to be unafraid if you are being asked to sell your company. Selling your business in Europe is often regarded as a sign that somehow you failed in your ability to create value. It's often a false sign. Selling a company may be the right thing for it; sale doesn't necessarily mean you failed.

On the issue of valuation, you have to be realistic, recognizing that most valuations are relative. You therefore need a thorough understanding of your comparables, or comparative companies, and how you compare with them. Adopting a realistic approach to your company's valuation will help avoid disappointment.

When it's time for an exit, be ready, and be flexible.

Mark Clement joined Merlin in March 2000. A Chartered Accountant and Fellow of the Securities Institute he has over 17 years corporate finance experience with Price Waterhouse Coopers, ABN AMRO, Hoare Govett, and West LB Panmure. In 1992 he was co-founder and Finance Director of Celsis International Plc. He has extensive experience in negotiating and managing collaborations and consolidations both in the US and in Europe. He is a non-executive director of investee companies of the Merlin Biosciences Fund and of the Merlin General Partner II Ltd.

Successful Exit Strategies

Peter Roberts

General Partner
Longworth Venture Partners

Investment Strategies

We invest in enterprise software, infrastructure software and technology-enabled business services and expect to be invested in a company anywhere from three to seven years (even though holding periods during the bubble were shorter). Occasionally, if a company has leading edge technology in a new market that is particularly attractive to a strategic partner, we have exited investments within a year. We had that happen with a company that was developing its product on the front end of the e-commerce craze and more recently with a storage-related company. Both were acquired within four months of our investment. The state of the IPO market can have a big impact as well. When the markets had a big appetite for IPOs between 1997 and 1999, some of the companies we invested in went public within 18 or 24 months of the initial investment. Since the IPO window closed after 2000, we have been in some companies for four or five years. The M&A market slumped as well as the value and performance of potential acquirers fell.

In applying the lessons learned through these cycles to the future, the only real strategy as it relates to exits is to make sure you invest in good companies in the first place and keep them focused on operating performance. We're kidding ourselves if we think we have a definite exit strategy that we can control. You have to really look at the fundamentals. If a company is a leader in its market, steadily grows its revenues and becomes profitable, it will gain some control over its own destiny. Such valuable companies often are approached by a suitor or have a public offering opportunity.

In a normal venture capital marketplace, we are more likely to sell our companies. That is, as a company starts to develop momentum, builds a good list of customers and proves that it can win business from more established players, there is a good chance it will be approached to be acquired. Establishing good technology or distribution partnerships with potential acquirers improves that probability – they see the value created firsthand. It is much harder to put a company up for sale and control the timing of that sale process. If you do that, you are likely to lose a lot of value and hinder operating performance.

Role of the VC in the Exit Process

One of the companies that we had been invested in for two and a half years was making very good progress and was the leader in a very specific vertical marketplace. It provided enterprise class applications to municipal governments for public safety. It had grown steadily during that period, its revenues were up to over $60 million and it was profitable. Thus, it appeared to have the right characteristics to pursue a public offering. So, as the venture capitalists, we had a discussion with the management team at the board level to make sure they were aligned with that objective, that it made sense for them to run a public company and that the business model was mature enough to produce predictable quarterly performance.

Once we had broad agreement that it was the right thing to do for the business and it was the right time, we began introducing the management team to a variety of investment bankers to choose the one we thought understood our business the best, would be most dedicated to our process, and would consider us a leading client. We also wanted the one with the best research analysts, who would follow the company and keep investors informed of the progress. We brought in three or four investment banks, had them make their pitch and helped the management team select the final investment banker. We then coached them in writing their prospectus, going through the SEC filing process and ultimately completing a successful IPO. We were very actively involved.

In another case where a company was sold, management came to us and presented an offer they had received. They discussed the strategic rationale behind the buyer's interest in the company and told us what the buyer wanted to pay and how. In this case it was a stock deal. We had to evaluate whether or not we wanted that buyer's stock and coach management on the stock's illiquidity. We also discussed with them what we thought the likely outlook was for that acquirer in terms of the future value of the stock. We then participated with the management team to negotiate the terms and price of the deal.

Once the sale goes through, some of the management team stays on as employees of the new company. Quite often, the vesting of the stock that they receive in that transaction requires them to stay on board for the next year or two. They go through the process of integrating the companies and trying to maximize the value of the combined entity. The venture capitalists, if they're lucky enough to ultimately cash out of that transaction, go off and do the next deal. The lockup period on their stock will typically expire within six months.

When a company is being sold at a value that will result in a loss to the VCs and leaves no value in the options or stock ownership of the management team, the VCs will often create incentives for the management team to complete a transaction by providing them with a so-called "carve out." That means management is guaranteed a percentage of the proceeds even though that is not what they are entitled to by the underlying investor agreements.

Which Exit Strategy to Pursue

An IPO is the right exit strategy if you have a company that is the leader in its market, can sustain a substantial growth curve for a long period of time and has a stable product and happy customers. You also must believe that its business model is strong enough to be steady and predictable, because once companies go public, they have to produce strong quarterly revenue performance and earnings results in line with analyst expectations. Thus, venture-backed companies are more likely to be sold than they are to go public. In fact, it's not unusual for companies in the process of filing for public offerings to receive offers from suitors who are attracted by their performance.

The worst time to pursue an exit strategy is when you are nearly out of cash; unfortunately, that is when a lot of companies are put up for sale. The VCs, particularly over the past three years when companies have struggled with a poor environment, have been forced to sell struggling companies to avoid providing additional funding. However, selling a company typically takes six to nine months and enough funding to get through that period. Also, prospective buyers know that you do not have much leverage when running out of cash and take advantage of that.

Other Exit Options

One option a company can pursue is to find another private company interested in a merger. Sometimes two struggling companies in similar businesses can merge, eliminate some of the costs and live to see another day. That strategy is often unsuccessful and may lead to additional funding requirements. Another option is to wind down the business and pursue the sale of its intellectual property. A technology company that has developed unique technology and has copyrights or patents may also consider sale of just the technology or intellectual property.

Liquidity

Management teams should recognize that an IPO in itself is not a liquidity event for them. It is very unlikely that they will be able to sell a material amount of their stock in the public offering and will be under severe restraints from selling stock post offering. If management starts unloading their stock, public investors may start to panic. A public offering is a long-term commitment for the management team and carries significant personal burdens in the current environment of heavy scrutiny.

Venture capitalists also have to realize that going public is not an immediate liquidity event. Many venture capitalists own substantial positions in their companies and retain board seats post offering. Thus, they face many of the same issues as management as well as minimum "lockup" periods of 180 days. After the public offering, you have to be comfortable that the stock is going to continue to appreciate as stock sales are managed over a period of time based on SEC restrictions as well as general market conditions.

Stock for stock mergers also carry limitations on ability to sell, including lockup periods. In the event of a company sale in a cash transaction, some amount is typically held in escrow for at least a year. So-called "earnout" clauses may also defer payments pending certain future performance benchmarks.

Roles of Management

Management and the board of directors share fiduciary duties when exit opportunities arise. The decision point may arise because performance and market conditions open the opportunity for an IPO, because of an approach by a prospective buyer or because of under performance and cash constraints. The role of the CEO when approached by an acquirer is to first of all consider if it is a real offer, assess the viability of the prospective acquirer and determine whether the sale or merger makes sense. The CEO should quickly bring to the attention of the board any preliminary offer or indication of interest. It is important that the CEO understands his responsibility to inform the board when any such event occurs. With the concurrence and input of the board, the CEO should prepare a response to the approach and have his staff prepare for due diligence requests. At the same time, the CEO should make sure his team remains focused on successful operations and fend off distractions that may impair performance and value.

The most common mistake management teams make is taking their focus off of the business. It's easy to get caught up in the prospects of selling the business or going public. This could impact performance in the near term and put the transaction at risk and/or deflate the valuation. Continue to run the business as if the transaction is not going to happen.

Beyond the board and the CEO, the CFO carries a lot of the burden of preparing the responses to the due diligence requests, preparing alternative budge scenarios, managing the interface of the legal documentation, etc. The technology team is also very important. The buyer will typically grill the chief technology officer about the product and underlying technology. The vice president of engineering can also offer valuable information in terms of how the product has been developed, how it has been architected, how well documented it is and how well it can be upgraded and maintained.

Valuation

Valuation is an art, not a science. A big part of the valuation discussion is based on comparable company valuations, growth, profitability and the strategic value of the product or technology. At some point you may engage an investment banker to help identify both private and public companies that have comparable businesses and to apply alternative valuation approaches. Relative comparables of multiples of revenue and earnings are considered. Consider the growth rate of your business and its relative market position to see whether or not it deserves a premium over those comparable values.

Finding the Right Buyer

Most good companies develop close long-term relationships with certain partners for distribution, product development or other initiatives. Development of those relationships creates a natural group of potential suitors who are familiar with the company. If one does make an approach, you have the advantage of quickly qualifying that potential buyer in terms of capacity to pay, chemistry and cultural fit and likelihood of successful closure of a transaction. If you are performing well, the universe and quality of potential suitors grow, as does your leverage in negotiations. If the company is struggling, however, you are looking for whatever buyer you can find.

To attract a buyer in the future, develop good partnership relationships now. If approached, maintain leverage by remaining focused on performance and do your homework to drive discussions of what you are worth. What is your strategic value to the buyer and what projections are achievable given the benefits of a merger such as expanded distribution channels and cost savings? The suitor will look at its own list of comparable companies and come up with projections of what they think you can do in the future. Price is based on the perception of what the future will bring.

Advice

The best advice I can offer is to build a great business. If you do and it is profitable, the exit takes care of itself. In other words, the most successful exit strategy is to develop the best team, product and market opportunity that you can.

Remain focused on the goal of controlling your company's destiny and the timing of a sale or IPO by striving for profitability and being as efficient with the capital required to get there as you can. If you have to sell a company, initiate the process early enough to have plenty of cash to get through the process and to maintain leverage. This is a critical decision point for VCs. Is this the right time to give up and sell or do you have enough faith in the prospects of the business to burn through more cash and probably face dipping into your fund's pocket again? Sometimes the smartest thing to do is take your medicine and face reality for the sake of both investors and management. Drudging along in "the land of the living dead" is no fun for anybody.

Peter Roberts brings 12 years of senior partner level venture capital experience to Longworth. Following seven years in commercial banking, he joined BancBoston Ventures' London office in 1989. In 1993 he joined BancBoston Ventures' early stage IT team in Boston and led its software investments for 8 years.

During his tenure, he led and managed 25 investments including HTE, WayPoint, Internet Capital Group, Allaire, Silknet, Arbinet and WebCT. He continues to leverage his enterprise software domain expertise at Longworth.

The Various Stages of Investing

Bill McAleer
Managing Director
Voyager Capital

The Stages of Venture Capital Investing

As a venture capital firm, we evaluate exit horizons based on the stage at which we invest. The typical horizon in early stage investing is five to seven years. If we invest in what is called a mid-stage company, then it's probably three to five years. With later stage investments, the horizon is somewhere between one and three years.

A seed investment is typically the first venture money that comes into a company and is usually structured as a series A financing. Early stage venture firms invest in either series A or series B financing rounds, which are usually the first or second rounds of investment. Often a seed stage company is funded initially by the founder or what are called "angel investors." These are individual investors, sometimes friends or family of the founder. If it's a technology company, venture firms usually invest once a prototype of the product has been completed. The company ideally might have had some initial conversations with customers to test the product idea, but at that point, it is fairly early in the selling cycle. The size of the company might be between 5 and 15 people.

Typically, the overall returns in early stage investments are slightly better than the returns in mid- or later stage investing. There is also more risk involved early on because the product is less developed, the market is unproven and there is less certainty of success. In a mid-stage round, which could be a B, C or even a D round, you are looking at a shorter horizon for an exit because at this point, some of the market and product risk is mitigated. The company usually has revenue and several customers have implemented the product. At this point, the company is generally raising capital to secure more marketing and sales dollars, while in the earlier stages it is raising money to finish the product.

A later-stage investor is often investing in a company that has revenues of at least $3 or $4 million a quarter or more. Most have $10 to $15 million a year in annualized revenues. At that point, the company is approaching or at profitability, and it is usually looking for the last round of capital to take it to a public offering (IPO) or an exit of some sort. That time horizon is a lot shorter – usually between one and three years.

Companies typically raise more capital as they progress through later stages of raising capital. In other words, the further along a company is, the more you will be investing. From a return perspective, data from Thomson Financial indicates that returns for early-stage investors, over a 20-year period, were about 21 percent. For later-stage investors, it was about 14 percent. So, there is usually a little better return in early-stage investing, but there is a higher risk too, since there is a lot less proven about the business. At an early stage, there is product risk and market risk. If you invest at mid-stage, generally you have just marketing and sales risk. Because you typically can get a bigger percentage of the company in an early stage investment, you can get a much bigger return if you are successful.

Early Growth Strategies

At Voyager, we focus on building successful companies, and that is our first priority. We want to work on the fundamentals of the company, which will then make it attractive for either a merger and acquisition opportunity or an IPO. We focus our efforts at the board level in three areas, which we call "acceleration activities." The first is recruiting key team members, generally at the management level or the board. Second is business and market strategy. We have an affiliation with the Chasm Group, the premier technology marketing strategy firm and one of their partners is one of our venture partners. When we first invest, we offer his services to come in and help the company think about its target customers and go-to-market strategy, which is often where high-tech companies struggle.

The third area we spend time on is helping with customers and strategic partner introductions. With high-tech companies, once you have gone to market with a product and have a few customers, it is important to develop a few key strategic relationships. They could help you get better distribution, access to a market or recognition in a market. These strategic relationships, which could include partnering with another software company or a large integrator that you use to deploy your product, often help to accelerate the market penetration of a company. They could also turn into an M&A opportunity: As you work together and develop relationships, it can be attractive for the other company to acquire your product.

Having access to strong resources is another key factor in building a successful company. We help our companies expand their contact base, which may mean getting outside directors, for example. Several studies indicate that qualified and active outside directors can help accelerate a company's growth. In many cases, we also assist in recruiting an advisory board of industry expert analysts or customers to provide advice and support. These strategies can help create more exit options.

The Role of the Venture Capitalist in the Exit Strategy

There are generally three ways to exit a company. One is through a public offering and a small percentage of companies make it to that stage. The second is through a merger and acquisition, where a company is acquired or merges with another company. In some technology sectors right now, having sufficient scale is important to getting on the radar screens of the IT people in companies. The third and most unattractive option is going out of business, which is the least desired and most unsuccessful way.

The VC can be very active in the exit process because we have a time clock ticking on our investments, and we are conscious of the length of time we've been in an investment. The role can have multiple dimensions. We can help the team think through their options, make introductions to strategic partners and assist in negotiations. Once we have some interest from an acquirer, I suggest to CEOs that they stay out of the negotiations because they don't always do the best job of representing themselves. They do a good job of telling the story, but many CEOs are not well suited to negotiate M&A transactions. Especially in a situation where we want to keep the team on board after the acquisition, it is better if the CEO doesn't get involved. Too often, the CEO may get into a confrontational mode with the team of the acquiring company during the negotiations, which could be detrimental to their post-merger working relationships. My suggestion is if you have a strong CFO or board member, then have one of them take the lead in negotiating the deal points. The CEO can then play the good guy. He pitches the company and builds the relationship, but is not actively involved in the negotiations.

M&A vs. IPO

Both an M&A and an IPO can be excellent exit strategies. An acquisition is a little cleaner sometimes, particularly if it is an all-cash deal. Sometimes the premiums can be rather attractive, and the process may be shorter. In order to go public, a company is generally looking at a five- to seven-year cycle, but an M&A can occur at any point.

The best time for an M&A is when the company has good revenue growth prospects and/or is uniquely positioned with its technology. We've seen a couple of private companies that happened to be in the right place at the right time. In those cases, very substantial premiums – four to six times revenues or more – are paid for companies that have fairly minimal revenues, but have a product that is very unique. We often are seeing these multiples in the data center, storage and security markets at the current time. A number of private companies that specialize in security have been bought because the sector is consolidating.

Mergers and Acquisitions: The Process

Many M&A transactions tend to be opportunistic. The opportunities arise because the acquiring company has had some exposure to the target company's product or service. Many times those are the most successful exits because you don't have to go out in search of a buyer. The deal comes about as a result of relationships that the company has developed with the buyer.

Another way to get M&A activity going is when the company happens to be in the right space at the right time. As a result, it gets picked up by a bigger company to fill in its product line. The third way is to hire an advisor to assist in selling the company. That approach is most successful when you already have a potential buyer interested. Ideally, you use an advisor to help manage the process and get some other buyers to the table to create a competitive environment. That will bring you the best price. If you have only one buyer, you could obtain a reasonable premium if there is a specific need to fill in the acquirer's product line or market footprint.

IPO: The Process

In the tech business today, IPOs are a less common event, unlike the frothy environment in 1999-2000. We should ignore the bubble period when a lot of companies went public that shouldn't have – many of them were mid-stage companies that should have been funded by VCs.

In a normal IPO market there are certain criteria that bankers look for. Typically, the company would have one to three quarters of profitability, good quarter-over-quarter growth -- usually in excess of 25 percent to 30 percent -- and year-to-year growth of 50 percent to 75 percent or better. Good growth momentum is critical before you take it public.

In addition to the company having a very unique market opportunity, a high-quality management team is important. A company must have an experienced team, particularly a CEO who is effective in talking to investors and, ideally, a strong CFO as well. It is also good to have a board that is comprised of experienced outside directors.

Once the board, in conjunction with the management team and the investors, decides it is time for an IPO, it begins a search for an investment banker. That process can be as lengthy or short as the company wants it to be, but generally several investment bankers should be brought in to evaluate the company. An ideal banker has strong analyst coverage in the company's sector and knowledge of potential competitors. If possible, you want to have two to three bankers on the financing, with one as the lead. The reason for that is to give the company more analyst coverage. It is important to have as many people following a company as possible when it goes public.

To choose an investment banker, you examine the firm's expertise in your market space, its reputation and its track record in taking companies public successfully and attracting the right institutional investors. Pricing is similar across the board, so that is usually not a distinguishing factor. At the end of the day, it is a combination of reputation, relevance and chemistry. You will be spending a lot of time with these people during the road shows, so you also want people who you can relate to pretty well.

The process of selecting a banker is called the "bake-off." You normally have three to five investment bankers give management and the board a pitch on what they think the valuation can be, the size of the offering, the scope of their reach with institutional investors and the quality of their analyst coverage. With the new regulations, we see fewer analysts in the process. It used to be you'd have the bankers and the analysts showing up together, but now it is often just the bankers, so you have to check out the analysts as part of the process as well.

After you have picked the banker, you negotiate the terms of the offering, which are fairly standard. You will negotiate the lockup period –who will be locked up and for how long, (six months is standard) and the size of offering. Valuation can be a factor. There may be bankers that propose significantly larger valuations and others that don't, and you will need to assess what is a realistic range.

Once the investment banking syndicate is selected, you then bring your attorneys and bankers together for an organizational meeting, and you are off to the races. In the first meeting, you agree to a schedule of activities. The typical time frame from start to finish of an IPO is between three and four months depending on the extent of SEC review.

The first step is to prepare the offering document, which is drafted by your attorneys with the investment banker counsel, the CFO and sometimes the CEO. It can be quite time consuming and a couple of all-nighters are not unusual.

Then you file the offering. There is usually a one-month comment period for that filing and once you respond to the SEC, then the road show to investors begins. These are generally twelve-hour days of meetings with investors. That can take one to three weeks, depending on coverage demand and how big the offering is. Once that is finished, final SEC clearance is obtained, and then the bankers get together and decide how to price the deal. Usually the attorneys are involved in a meeting or pricing phone call with the management and the board.

In pricing an IPO, the bankers look at comparable public companies, and compare at what point those companies went public in their sector. That is how they initially determine the pricing range, and that's what they pitch to management. But after the road show, what determines the price is how much demand there is for the stock. That can be somewhat different than what was represented when the bankers were trying to sell the deal. CEOs have to be realistic about what the bankers tell them. Sometimes the bankers whisper a lot of sweet things in their ears that don't ever come true. I think it is good to have experienced board members or VCs because a lot of us have heard the promises before, and we can gauge reality based on our prior experience.

The board then approves the pricing of the offering, and the company goes public. The first trading day is accompanied by lots of champagne and celebrations with your employees. The next stage for most companies is getting used to being in the public market. You need to do quarterly reporting and ensure that the proper control systems are in place for SEC and Sarbanes-Oxley compliance. The preparation for going public starts a year or two ahead of time. I always encourage my companies to implement proper management disciplines during that period, particularly as it relates to financial reporting disclosures and communication with employees. These processes must be in place because the company will be under a lot of scrutiny once it is public.

After the company goes public, the venture capitalists will generally stay on the board for a period of time. Most of the VCs transition off the board once they have sold their positions. The VCs are generally locked up for six months, as are most of the investors. That means no one can distribute or sell their stock during that time. Most VCs distribute stock in an orderly way; usually they sell 30 percent to 40 percent of their position after the lockup period expires and they then distribute one or two more pieces, depending on how much of the company they own. Firms with smaller holdings usually distribute more immediately following the lockup period.

The board of directors is accountable to the shareholders while the company passes into the early stages of adulthood after it goes public. It is important to achieve predictability in your business, which is often difficult for tech companies. Just about every public tech company, other than perhaps Microsoft, has had some hiccup at some point in their development.

What we see is interesting. Companies generally go public when they have between $50 million and $75 million per year in revenues. As they grow, there are usually inflection points at about $100 million and another one at about $200 million where they must make changes so they will continue to grow.

Best Market Conditions for Selling a Company

As mentioned earlier, you ideally want a market that is perceived as being hot by the public or the investment sector. For instance, right now, security and storage are fairly hot, and the multiples for private companies in those areas are fairly high – in the fives and sixes. That's because there is a consolidation occurring and a much stronger market need. Also, you want the company to be showing good revenue growth, experiencing strong product traction with initial customers or to have a very unique product. Strong positive momentum is not always what sells because sometimes a company may have choppy revenue or performance, but happens to be in the right market space.

During 2000, one of our companies had a very unique product in the streaming media space, and there was only one competitor. We had a long conversation with the CEO to determine whether we should fund the company for another round or sell the company because the CEO was getting some feelers from companies with whom he had developed strategic relationships. In one case, a marketing partner wanted to offer a broader product footprint. We anticipated that the market space was going to consolidate and our portfolio company was in an early stage with fairly low revenues, but, again, it was a unique product in a hot market. We decided with the CEO that we should go ahead and sell to the strategic partner, instead of giving it another round of funding. We hit right at the top of the market and got very good returns. That is an example of where we sold a company very early with great timing – we had been in the investment less than two years and made seven times our investment.

Valuation

There are three traditional ways to value a company, and what you use depends on the maturity of the company. One is the use of comparable valuation multiples, a second is to look at specific transactions and the third is the net present value (NPV) method.

Under the comparable method, we identify other public companies in the company's market sector and compare their revenue multiples or their price/earnings ratios. With earlier stage companies, we tend to focus on revenue multiples. In more mature companies, we usually consider earnings multiples. From the comparable companies, we develop a beta range and an average – a median or mean. Then, you discount those for a private company anywhere from 20 percent to 40 percent, depending on the stage of the company – the earlier the stage, the higher the discount. For example, if you have $5 million in revenues, and the multiple for revenues were three, you apply a discount of, say, 30 percent to get a 2.1 multiple. You apply that to your revenue number and that gives you a valuation of approximately $10 million. That provides one reference point.

The second approach is to look at private company transactions. For companies that have been funded, we try to research at what price they were funded. There are sources like Venture One that details the company's funding history. In some cases, they report revenues and in other cases, they report their valuations. There may be five or six similar companies, and we do an average and see how it compares. In a more mature business, we use a third method, a discounted (NPV) cash flow analysis. You take the projected cash flows and discount them at a risk-adjusted rate of capital to determine a valuation range based on the discounted cash flow.

A final way to value a company is to consider the valuation relative to the market capitalization of the acquiring company, and then determine what your percentage of that company will be after the acquisition. For example, let's say the selling company's revenues are $10-$15 million and the acquirer's revenues are $70 million. The selling company has $10 million, so it should represent, post-merger, 10/80 of the combined revenues. This ratio would then be applied to acquirer's market capitalization to estimate the selling company's valuation. All of these valuation reference points can be used to develop a range of values to negotiate from.

Getting the Best Deal

In summary, it is important to create a competitive environment for pricing by having more than one potential acquirer look at the company. You also want to make sure to put your best foot forward in terms of what you present to the buyer and to be organized in how you do that. Buyers are interested in future revenue streams as well as what the company has done in the past, so it is important to be able to show that you have a strong product vision that the two companies could execute together. It is also important to show that there is revenue momentum in your business. Your revenue pipeline or the number and quality of the customers you have, the segments the customers are in and how that matches with the acquirer's segments are also important. Think about what the two companies look like together, and appeal to whatever the acquirer's hot buttons are for acquisition, be it technology, customers or product line expansion. It's a selling opportunity, so you have to emphasize the points that are most compelling to the buyer.

Deal Structure

There are three basic structures. One is an all-cash transaction, where the buyer acquires the assets or stock of the selling company for cash. In that case, you may care as much about the buyer other than whether they can pay. In this situation, you look at how to get the best realization for the investors and the management team. The best buyer is a company with significant cash that has made acquisitions before and knows the process.

The second type is a stock transaction. In this situation, you need to spend time looking at how the team is going to fit in the acquiring company and how the product offering contributes to its overall revenue stream. Is it a solid company in good financial condition and growth prospects? Make sure that the acquirer has a compelling product strategy that allows you to continue to grow the business after the acquisition. If the company has completed acquisitions before, that's good because it understands how to integrate companies. A lot of work has to go into the integration effort to make it successful after the merger.

The third structure is an earn out, where consideration in stock or cash is paid upfront, combined with additional consideration that is paid when certain financial goals (generally revenue or profit) are met and this type of structure is designed to influence the entrepreneur to stay and grow revenues for a year or two after the acquisition. In that situation, you need to understand how much independence the entrepreneur will have to hit their targets. In addition, you want to be sure there is a clear definition of what the earn out is based on, that the team can influence the results tied to earn out. Earn outs can be difficult because sometimes the acquirer will make significant changes, such as gutting the sales force to the surviving organization. Then the seller can't hit their earn out numbers. Hence, in an earnout situation, it is important to clearly define the basis for the earn out and the post-acquisition structure that will be in place to ensure that the earn out can be achieved.

The Shut Down Scenario

In managing the company, it is important for any management team to align their objectives with their venture capitalists or their board. Be clear on what milestones have to be accomplished by the time you do your next round of funding.

We had a portfolio company where we agreed with the management team on three milestones they had to meet and mutually set them. One was a revenue milestone, one was a product milestone and the third was a customer milestone. We funded the company and indicated that we would re-fund them if they could reach those objectives. Unfortunately, we came to the end of their funding, and the company had met only one of the three objectives. We told them we were sorry, but we couldn't continue to fund them. The management team understood our position – they knew they hadn't made their goals. It was painful, but at least people walked away knowing we had been fair because the expectations were clear.

As a venture capitalist, you have to continually watch the horizon and work with the management team to understand when they will be out of cash, and if they miss a quarter, ensuring that the team has a contingency plan.

If you decide to shut down the company, there is a point where the board and the VCs as directors have a fiduciary responsibility to ensure that the liabilities are satisfied – in particular, employee liabilities, tax liabilities and secured lenders. The investors and entrepreneurs must ensure that there is enough cash to take care of those in a satisfactory way. Then, the creditors take whatever is left of the company. Someone from the board or a former management team member has to wrap up things, resolve all the liabilities and may have to file for Chapter 13 or 11, if necessary. Sometimes out of the ashes comes a recapitalization of the company where one or two of the founders decide to buy the technology out of bankruptcy and start over again.

Most Frequent Mistakes by Entrepreneurs during an Exit

In an acquisition situation, the first mistake is to prolong the conversation with a potential acquirer. The seller may get the right signals from a company they are talking to, and the negotiation goes all the way down to the end and then the acquirer walks away or runs the company out of cash to the point where it can buy it at a significant discount. Entrepreneurs are optimistic by nature, and the second mistake they make is to be too optimistic about acquisition conversations. It is important to get a good idea about whether the buyer is serious or not.

The third mistake is when the entrepreneur negotiates his own deal. Some CEOs are not well equipped to negotiate a transaction. They haven't had the experience, they don't know how to shop it and they don't recognize positioning points. CEOs should get help from a board member, an experienced CFO or an outside advisor. Many times, ego gets in the way in negotiations.

When I was at Aldus, we merged with Adobe, which was a half-billion dollar merger. At the time, in the early 1990s, it was the largest deal ever announced in the software industry. We consciously came up with a strategy to have our CEO work with the CEO of Adobe and then we hired an investment banker, as they did, and had the investment bankers manage most of the negotiations with the two CFOs. The CEOs worked together on the vision and objectives – the fundamentals of the merger – rather than negotiating terms. That way, the principals were involved in discussing the future and the acquirer was more enthusiastic about paying up for the deal.

For an IPO, CEOs make the mistake of thinking they have to be the primary investor interface, and after the company goes public, they become enamored with talking to investors and being the center point for investor activity. That doesn't scale very well. After the IPO, you should get back to managing the company and let your CFO handle the ongoing investor relations.

Another IPO related mistake is to become mesmerized by what the investment bankers are telling them and getting their valuation expectations out of line compared to reality. A third mistake is when an entrepreneur does not understand what needs to be in place after the company goes public, such as management disciplines and processes. The best way to learn about such things is to talk to others who have taken companies public. Talk to your attorney, your board and other advisors.

In a headed for shutdown scenario, the biggest problem is a sense of optimism that you will make it through, and failing to realize that the performance isn't there.

Advice to Management Teams

Number one is to focus your business for the long term and on the fundamentals. Number two is to work on developing strategic relationships that potentially create leveraged customer opportunities or exit options for you. Number three, try to resist on negotiating the deal if you have other people you can rely on to do it.

A co-founder of Voyager, Bill McAleer has extensive executive and equity financing experience in the technology industry. Bill has participated on the boards of 15 companies, including nine portfolio companies, focusing on enterprise software, data center solutions, digital media, and wireless services. Three portfolio companies, Amplitude, Netpodium, and Tegic, were sold, and he currently serves on the boards of Kadiri, Melodeo, RackSaver, SeeCommerce and Austin-based ClearCommerce. He also sits on the board of Avocent (NASDAQ: AVCT), a public company with over $260 million in revenues.

Prior to Voyager, Bill was president of e.liance Partners, advising information technology companies on strategy, venture financing, and corporate partnering from 1994 to 1996. Between 1988 and 1994, Bill served as vice president of finance, CFO, and secretary of Aldus, when the company's revenues grew from $39 to $240 million. He was responsible for global finance, legal, operations, and business development activities, including completing the merger with Adobe in 1994. Prior to Aldus, Bill was a vice president with Westin Hotels.

Bill is active in several industry organizations such as the EVCA, Financial Executives Institute, and the WSA. He is also advisory board member for the University of Washington Center for Technology and Entrepreneurship and Cornell University's Johnson Graduate School of Business. He has been a featured speaker at industry conferences and panels. He also serves as a director for Big Brothers Big Sisters. He earned a B.S. and an MBA from Cornell University.

Steps to Exiting an Investment

Stephen J. Warner
Chairman & Founder
CrossBow Ventures

Exiting an Investment

The most common way to exit an investment is a merger with another company in the industry or a sale to a larger company in the same industry. A second type of exit is a sale to a financial buyer such as an LBO fund. Another way to exit an investment is through a public offering and subsequent sale in the public market. Finally, most deals have provisions for ultimate redemption or buyback of the investor's securities by the company, but that is a relatively rare occurrence.

The timeline we are looking at in terms of exiting a position after we make an investment is typically three to six years. Some of the variables that may affect that timing are the stage of the company when we invest and the market conditions at the time when the company has reached a point where we may consider exiting. The earlier we invest in a company, the longer it takes for the company to mature to a point where we can realize value on an exit.

We have to consider the position of the business and its prospects in light of the opportunities for an exit in terms of market conditions and interest from potential buyers. If we exit too early, we could leave a lot of potential on the table and if we wait too long, we may miss the market opportunity. It is also affected by who is doing the exiting. For example, a venture fund is typically a 10-year partnership. Venture managers want to exit sometime before a partnership is up, so they are not in a position to hold for 15 years.

The worst time to pursue an exit strategy is when the market is depressed and the industry is out of favor. Nobody will value the company very highly at that point. We are not going to realize much value. Another bad time would be when the company is taking off and we would miss the major value increase by exiting too early.

The best time to exit a venture investment is when the company has fully validated its business model, defined the market for its product or service and has established a measurable growth trend. If this stage of the business coincides with favorable market conditions where the particular industry or technology has a high level of investor interest, these conditions can lead to exceptional exit values either from competing industry buyers or an IPO.

Mergers and Sales

There are two major types of mergers and sales. One is where the buyer initiates contact with the company it wants to acquire. In those cases, the process is one of a lot of meetings and due diligence by the buyer and negotiations on the part of the company to be bought. Frequently an investment banker will act as a go between or facilitator. If there is a venture syndicate, there is often considerable positioning, posturing and negotiating among the various venture investors. Ultimately, if everyone can agree on the values and the legal issues are resolved, then the sale or merger takes place.

The other major situation is where the company initiates the process by contacting people in the industry to see if anyone is interested in buying it. An investment banker representing the company is frequently used in that process. Once the interest is developed on the part of the potential buyers, the process is pretty similar to the above.

A sale to a financial buyer differs in the sense of what the parties are most sensitive to. If it is an industry buyer, they are looking at synergies and opportunities to combine functions and cut costs, and gauging the effects on markets and customers. A financial buyer is simply looking at the company as an investment. It is usually a simpler process with a financial buyer in that there are not as many issues. On the other hand, it is sometimes more complicated in that a financial buyer may not have an understanding of the industry or the business, so there is more of an education process involved.

The very best terms are achieved when there is more than one interested party. You then can make the negotiation for the seller much easier because you can play potential buyers against each other. If there is not a competing buyer, it is more difficult to maximize your value; you have to convince the buyer that it is in his best interest to pay a higher price. That is done by putting the company up for sale in the best light in terms of what its potential and future looks like and how it will enhance the potential buyer.

The best buyers are ones to which the selling company brings a distinct and identifiable value. It may bring the buyer to a new market or a new segment of customers, it may provide a complementary line of business or it might offer potential for considerable cost savings by combining functions. So that's what we look for first. If a company cannot find a buyer at all, there is the option of liquidation or selling off pieces or assets. That is usually not very satisfactory. A better option is to get back to work and figure out how to make the company attractive so that it can be sold.

IPOs

An IPO is usually the right exit strategy when it can be done. It will usually result in the best price one can obtain for a deal as long as the market is receptive to that particular kind of business. However, it is frequently not possible to do an IPO for venture-backed companies. The stars all have to be right. The company has to be at the right stage and the market has to be at the right stage and have the right interest. You have to have the right coverage by the right analysts.

In an exit through an IPO, an investment banker gets involved and commits to working with a company and developing the offering. It is a highly regulated process, so it is lawyer-intensive. The first step is due diligence by the investment banker. The investment banker needs to understand the company and help develop the prospectus and disclosure information. Accountants are involved because there are a number of financial statements that appear in the prospectus that they have to sign off on.

The investment banker then proceeds to build a syndicate by inviting other investment banks to underwrite and sell part of the deal. The prospectus is filed with the SEC, and there is a period of several weeks where the SEC reviews the prospectus, gives comments back to the lawyers and underwriters including any deficiencies with respect to the disclosure form or format. Those are then addressed in an appropriate way until the SEC signs off on it. The deal is then free to be released. The night before the offering, after the close of the market, the deal is priced based on the market conditions at the close of that business day and then offered the next morning.

Determining how much of the company to sell to the public is usually a function of price and capital needs by the company as well as the ability of the underwriter to place or sell the issue. The underwriters typically want the size of the offering to be within a certain range that they are comfortable with and that they can place and still leave some demand unmet. They don't want it to be so small that it isn't worth their while or disappoints too many customers, so all that goes into the underwriters' comfort range. You need that range to cover the needs of the company for capital, which frequently are not all that specific. That determines what percent of the company you sell in order to hit the range and raise the money you need.

Typically in an IPO, the underwriters require what is called a lockup, meaning that all of the insiders – the management, directors and private investors – agree not to sell their stock for at least six months and sometimes a year. Management itself has additional restrictions that only allow them to sell during certain periods that relate to when they issue reports. The venture capitalists are usually in the same position with respect to the lockup period, but not as restricted as management once the lockup is over. Unless the venture capitalists are still on the board of directors, they can sell once the lockup is over. There are exceptions to that. Sometimes the public offering will include some stock that is held by either the venture capitalists or the management, but that is not very common.

Another situation that could happen is when there is still a great deal of demand for the stock a few months or so after the initial public offering. In that case, there could be a secondary public offering that would involve selling shares of the insiders in a registered, underwritten offering.

Roles of the VC and CEO in Exit Strategies

The role of the VCs when pursuing an exit strategy varies. They might take on a simple advisory role, helping the company choose the right investment banker or the right exit strategy whether it be a merger or trade sale or IPO. The VCs might also be extremely proactive. For instance, when a company is initiating the search for a trade buyer, the venture capitalists likely have contacts with companies in that industry and can make introductions and get involved in the negotiations.

The CEO's primary role is to continue running the company as best he can. He will undoubtedly be involved in any negotiations and in answering questions and providing the information on all of the due diligence work, though much of the due diligence would fall to the CFO. The CEO could be involved in identifying the potential buyers based on his relationships in the industry. The board ultimately makes the decision as to when and how and on what terms the exit or sale takes place. Company counsel would be involved in all the documentation.

Valuing the Company

When valuing the company, the most common approach is a comparables approach. That involves looking at the value of public companies in the same business or recent merger transactions with companies in the same business, and comparing those values as a function of sales, earnings, growth rates or number of customers. There are various metrics and measures that different businesses use. Ratios are developed on those measures and compared to companies that have an established value either in a public market or because of transactions or private sales. Sometimes investment bankers or others are hired to make these valuations, but they also start with the comparables and then give their opinions on which companies are comparable and how the subject company may differ and why it should be higher or lower based on the same metrics.

Bankruptcy and Liquidation

Bankruptcy can occur in two ways. In most cases, it is voluntary. The board decides to file for bankruptcy protection in order to hold off creditors while the company reorganizes or prepares to liquidate. The other way bankruptcy can occur is when the creditors get together and force the company into bankruptcy. If a company runs out of cash and is forced to sell, that is often the scenario in which there is a company-initiated bankruptcy. The company files for court protection against the creditors while it can organize itself to sell its assets or reorganize with a new plan. Typically that involves raising additional money.

Completion of an Exit Event

Generally all of the selling interests are all handled simultaneously at the closing of the deal. It is determined ahead of time who will get what. All the money or stock (proceeds of the sale) initially goes to the lawyers, typically in an escrow arrangement. The lawyers then distribute the proceeds of the sale as appropriate. The dividing of monies is usually determined by the structure of the company's capitalization. If we are talking about the sale of assets for cash so that all the assets go to the buyer, the company receives the cash and pays off all of its creditors and debt holders first, and then it goes to preferred stockholders in order of their liquidation preference. Whatever is left is divided up among the common stockholders. The lawyers and anyone else who has earned a fee for creating the sale gets their cut off the top.

If the purchase price ends up below original value, the common stockholders are the first to be out of luck. If there is only enough to pay off the debt and half the preferred shareholders, then that is what happens. The preferred shareholders lose half their value and the common stockholders get nothing. If there is not enough to even pay off all the debt, then none of the equity holders get anything. There are sometimes instances where the debt holders agree to take, say, 80 cents on the dollar so that the preferred shareholders can get something. That could happen when the preferred shareholders would not agree to the sale in the first place, knowing they would get nothing. In order to get some money from the deal, the debt holders might negotiate something like this.

Advice

One of the most frequent mistake entrepreneurs make is not pursuing an exit opportunity when available. The entrepreneur tends to be the last one interested in an exit because he has an emotional stake in the company and often feels that he can continue to build and do better. An exit will probably change his life drastically, and he may even lose his job. It is not just a financial issue for the entrepreneur; it is a lifestyle. One of the things venture capitalists do is to make sure that the entrepreneurs are interested in exits and not seeking to build a family dynasty that they can pass on to their children. Entrepreneurs must make sure they look beyond just their role and consider what is best for the company.

Another important factor is to keep the company and the books clean and make sure that the audits are done regularly and that there aren't deals or situations that would be embarrassing when disclosed. Ultimately they will have to be disclosed in an exit scenario.

Golden Rule of Successful Exit Strategies

In general, exits are the least controllable part of venture investing because they are so much a function of the marketplace and what is going on at the time. The most important part of an exit strategy is to keep an awareness of the opportunities available and keep the company in a position where it can take advantage of them when one presents itself. You need to be prepared.

Stephen J. Warner is the founder and chair of CrossBow Ventures a management company for $160MM of venture capital funds, including Crossbow Private Equity Partners LP and Crossbow Venture Partners LP, a Federally licensed SBIC.

From 1994 to 1998 he was chairman for Bioform Inc., a company for private equity investments and advisory services. He was a consultant to the U.S. Government on the evaluation of American Enterprise funds in Eastern Europe and capital markets projects in the Philippines. From 1991 to 1993 he was Managing Director for Commonwealth Associates. At Merrill Lynch & Co he founded and served as the President/CEO for 10 years of Merrill Lynch Venture Capital Inc. which managed over $250MM and directly participated in over 100 investments in venture capital situations. He served on advisory boards of several other venture funds in the U.S. and Europe. Earlier positions at Merrill Lynch included investment banking and Managing Director of Finance and Administration.

He received his B.S. from the Massachusetts Institute of Technology in 1962 and his MBA from the Wharton Graduate School of Business, University of Pennsylvania, in 1966.

Exiting Venture-Backed Companies: Merger, Acquisition, or IPO?

Bart Schachter
Founding & Managing Partner
Blueprint Ventures

Defining the Two Humps

My firm invests in seed and early-stage venture capital, so our window is long – from three to seven years. We view the exit timeline as a two-humped camel of traditional venture capital valuation. The early pre-revenue valuation and possible exit is based on the team assembled, the idea, the prognosis of market space, the vision, and the enthusiasm of the team – a somewhat artificial valuation but one that has seen many successful start-ups achieve. We saw this phenomenon frequently during the tech boom, when companies were being acquired quickly or just being formed for vast sums of money based on the number of engineers or their "time-to-market" advantage. More recently, pre-revenue exits persist in semiconductor companies where intellectual property ("IP") is often viewed as vitally important even for start-ups that have not yet shipped product.

With the second hump of the camel, real profitability, revenues, profitability growth, and cash flow become relevant. This is the more traditional valuation.

Venture-backed companies go through this two-humped-camel valuation process. The trick for us (and for entrepreneurs) is to figure out whether to sell out on the first hump or the second hump – but to avoid selling out in the valley of death. Entrepreneurs (and their venture capitalists) often fail to see the valley of death that follows immediately after the first hump. Silicon Valley is replete with stories of entrepreneurs that passed up an early acquisition offer (the first hump), hoping for greater value down the road. Instead, they never reached the second hump; they died in the valley of death. Rarely can a company reach the second hump, and when it does (3-5 years after the first) investors may find the valuation exactly the same as during the first hump. Because venture capital rewards investors on the basis of IRR (internal rate of return), the value of time has a potent deleterious effect on IRR – the same valuation is worth a lot more early on than it is during the second hump (if and when it arrives)

This is not to say that investors should rush to take the first offer that comes along. It means simply that we need to be aware of these two humps and monitor progress of our private companies.

We believe that exit valuations for successful venture-backed companies will be in the range of $100 million to $200 million for the foreseeable future. An exit for an amount in that range is the mark of a successful company. The challenge is how and when to achieve it.

Start-up Valuations: Two Humps

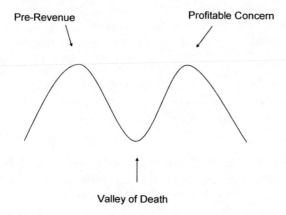

M&A vs. IPO

The two traditional exit strategies for venture-backed companies are M&A (merger and acquisition) and IPO (initial public offering). Over the past few years M&A has been the more common exit strategy. There have been few opportunities for IPOs over the last few years, although that is quickly changing in 2004 and beyond.

Our focus has been on the M&A market because it is robust and dependent. The M&A market has been more forgiving and doesn't follow the "windows" of public market offerings. In addition, and more arguably, the IRR of M&A exits is potentially more lucrative in a down market such as the one we have been experiencing.

The M&A market will always be robust as long as consumers and corporations continue their voracious appetite for technology and productivity gains. For the last few years, large corporations have been constrained by Wall Street from spending on "non-core" development or market creation concepts. Millions of employees have been laid off from Armonk, NY to Tokyo. Yet consumers continue to demand higher performance technology, better reliability, next-generation communications gear and more advanced consumer electronics. Suddenly, large companies find themselves unable to meet the demands of their core customers. Large telecommunications equipment companies, which for several years starved their "next-generation" development, are being asked to bid on projects for which they have no current technology. Consumers are demanding high-speed wireless home networks from their consumer-electronics suppliers, which also have been focused on quarter-to-quarter profitability and have largely ignored investment in these projects.

So once again, as in the mid-nineties, large companies (which successfully spent the last few years buttressing their balance sheets and income statements) are looking around to purchase other technology assets to fill out their product requirements and to fill holes in their product offerings. As a result they have to engage in the practice of purchasing companies as a matter of routine business evolution. This routine business evolution makes the M&A cycle a very reliable and consistent exit path for technology startups – subject acceptable valuations.

The IPO market is more fickle; it is prisoner to the cycle of Wall Street, when Wall Street feels it has significant interest in IPO companies. Fundamentally, no one actually needs an IPO and many economic factors lead to the opening and closing of public market "windows." As a new window opens in 2004, venture capital investors are finding that valuations for IPO companies are approaching those for successful M&As. In other words the IPO "premium" has all but disappeared except for the spectacular IPOs – Google often quoted in this category. Specifically, most venture-backed technology IPOs are settling into the $200M valuation range, which again falls into the expected range for *all* exits.

Many believe you should build every company to achieve an IPO, but that is not always the best strategy to follow. Let's say you have four to six quarters of profitability and can go either IPO or M&A. The path you take depends on the management group.

The most important differences between the two exit strategies are what happens to the management team and what their plans are for the business. Running a public company in today's market is very challenging and potentially hazardous because of compliance regulations, like the Sarbanes-Oxley Act and several other regulatory impasses. Many managers dislike the idea of running a public company because of the huge overhead it creates. The same holds true for venture investors who risk the possibility of becoming pawns in the regulatory game. This is a very time-consuming and unprofitable pastime for venture investors whose primary job is to make money for their limited partners. For the management team, the M&A and IPO paths are very different lifestyle choices. M&A promises fairly quick returns, minimal lockup periods, and potentially interesting work under the umbrella of a larger organization. Many an entrepreneur acquired by Cisco has successfully used a year or two exposure to that company to dream up the next idea for a start-up and go out once again to raise money and exploit it.

An IPO is often a more alluring exit yet it is fraught with uncertainty. Beyond the regulatory issues already described, managers are allowed to exit their holdings over a multi-year period during which they must be more focused then ever on building their business. Wall Street is a lot less forgiving than Sand Hill Road. Many spectacular IPOs have fizzled as the stock trended towards zero before the management team (and investors) was able to even recoup their investment.

The board decides when to pursue an exit strategy. Venture capitalists play an important role because frequently they are the most sizable shareholders in the company. But the decision must be made in concert with the management team.

M&A Process

The M&A process is one of identifying the timing for beginning the M&A and agreeing with your co-investors and management team that it is the right approach to take. Those are fundamentally the most important decisions. Once you decide to exit and to follow the M&A exit strategy, the next steps involve answering the following the questions:

- Do you engage investment bankers?
- Do you directly approach your target companies?
- Do you work through your business development channels?
- Do you approach the CFO of a target acquirer?

It is most important to agree at the board level on what the objectives of the discussion are and whether to engage investment bankers or another group to represent the company to potential buyers.

An M&A transaction is often the result of a prior business transaction between two companies. There is a saying in our business that companies are bought, not sold. Once a business relationship exists, a larger company will make an offer to buy a smaller company, but buying cannot be forced.

Some contest the use of investment bankers, while others think it is wise, and others are indifferent. Certainly it is better, if possible, to have an organic relationship with a potential buyer, which initiates through some business relationship. However, investment bankers can play an important role in management in the M&A process. Sometimes, even when an organic buyer exists, a good investment banker can help bid up the price by presenting the company to multiple or other buyers. The job of the board is to maximize the value of the business and using investment bankers can accomplish this goal. Other times, investment bankers can help expose a nascent start-up to potential acquirers outside their immediate scope. For example, overseas buyers can be attracted to bid on a start-up, once again maximizing the value of the company.

To develop an early relationship with a potential buyer, a start-up must develop those relationships early. For example, the board must identify early on potential acquirers and begin to develop those relationships years before a possible exit. Co-marketing, OEM, and co-development channels are an important way to begin the M&A process...before anybody would consider it a process at all.

IPO Exit Strategy

The IPO process is more formal and generally more expensive. It usually needs to start a year or more before the actual event. The process has been hampered over the last few years because there has been no window for IPOs.

The number one thing for a company to understand is that it is "IPO or bust." While an M&A transaction can always happen because the result is just a matter of agreeing on price, in today's market the criteria for an IPO are strict.

Only companies with four to six quarters of growth profitability are eligible for the public markets today. Companies can't go public on concepts; you must show you are a viable company with profitable results. So the first prerequisite is to make sure you fit as a company into the requirements for going public. If you cannot, then IPO is not an option.

The process that culminates in going public is one in which you engage, usually, with investment bankers and institutional buyers 12 to 15 months ahead of time. That means starting to court investment banker relationships and speak at investment banker forums, so that by the time you go public, your company is well known by potential buyers.

In an IPO, the lockup period lasts six to nine months for management. The goal is to show the purchasers of the stock that the insiders still care. A management sell-out on the first day would provide a sense that the investors are not aligned. You need to hold onto the management team for years, possibly longer, to ensure there is still good work going on in the company.

Legally, the VC can liquidate as early as the lockup period is over. Even after an IPO, it is likely the investors still own 75 percent of the company. If all the investors sold at once, that would depress the stock significantly. What generally happens after the lockup periods ends is that VCs start to gradually sell their holdings, around 5 percent a month, often taking several years. Sometimes, secondary public offerings are staged. These Wall Street offerings allow inside owners to sell some, though generally not all, of their holdings.

Determining the Value of an IPO Offering

There are some general historical numbers on how public companies are sold. Investment bankers provide some guidance. Usually companies offer in the 25 percent range: The company will float 25 percent of its ownership to the public and allow insiders to sell additional equity in what is called a secondary transaction 6 to 12 months after the IPO.

The decision on how much of the company to sell to the public is influenced more heavily by the suggestion of the investment banker than by anything else. The key point is to ensure that the retail or institutional investors who buy the public stock feel the insiders still have significant "skin in the game," in terms of their ownership. You want to leave enough in the company that confidence is built, but also start achieving liquidity for your investors.

The valuation is generally set on comparables – more or less a kind of science that compares what other public companies are trading for in a similar space and with similar kinds of revenue numbers. You want to look at companies that have a comparable set of economic characteristics: companies that are relatively young and in the same revenue range of your company; companies in the same space, like other software companies; companies with similar business models; and companies that target the same clients your company targets.

Valuation resembles pricing a piece of real estate: You find other pieces that have sold recently for similar amounts to determine the value of your land – or your company. The only way to know what your company is worth is to see what similar companies are worth.

The Best Time to Pursue an Exit Strategy

You want to sell a company when you can. As we have seen over the last few years, the assumption that tomorrow may bring a better price is not necessarily true. Many stories from the tech bubble tell of offers to buy a company for a half-billion dollars, but the owners did not want to sell and went bankrupt a year later. The conclusion that can be drawn is that the best time to sell a company is when you can. This brings us back to the double humped camel model.

For an IPO, the best time is not in your hands. The IPO window opens and shuts quickly. Right now there is a brief IPO window for biotech companies. We are expecting additional IPO windows to open – for example, once Google goes public, a number of technology companies will follow suit.

In the M&A market, timing is less important – maximum value is the driver. The M&A market timing has more to do with the company's prospects and alternatives. Acquirers are always trying to buy companies, so the object is for sellers to match those opportunities. M&A is all about cash. If a company feels it is on the top of one of those camel humps, it is probably a good time to sell. If the company is in the valley or moving off the top, selling is more treacherous.

The worst time to sell a company is when you are running out of cash and you do not have a choice. It's best to have choices and options. The board should make sure the company can choose whether to go public or to do an M&A – or whether to sell now or later. The board has to make these decisions at the right time. Giving up the bird in the hand for one in the bush at the wrong time can be disastrous.

Best Exit Strategy for VCs

To some extent, the cleanest exit strategy is an M&A transaction. It allows the VCs to move on. You sell the company; the transaction closes; you're finished.

An IPO does not end the process. Many VCs will continue to stay involved with the company after the IPO, even though doing so is not their job. From a purely financial perspective, we could argue that M&A is best. But if we're building a franchise, IPOs do have their own appeal. Cisco, whose original venture capitalists remain on its board some 15 years after its IPO, has bought nearly one hundred companies backed by investors on its board. Certainly, when viewed from that perspective, having a public company "vacuum cleaner" has been a productive use of those board members' time.

People used to be enamored with the process of going public. However, because of all the regulatory issues surrounding IPOs, people have returned to focusing on M&A transactions.

Roles in an Exit Strategy

The role of the venture capitalist is to guide the board of directors and the shareholders toward the best outcome for their stock. Venture capitalists are board members who represent investors and the company. They have a subtle fiduciary duty to maximize the value of both the investors and the management team. The goal is to steer toward an exit that maximizes that value, creating as much value as possible for the investors and shareholders of the company. VCs monitor environmental conditions and help drive toward that exit. For the VCs, that is probably the most important role after creating the company.

The role of the CEO is to execute on the desires of the board. If the exit strategy is an IPO, the role of the CEO is to take the company public in that 12- to 18-month window and continue to run the company. The CEO also finds a buyer – often a difficult trick because in many acquisitions the CEO ends up without a role in the combined company. Even more challenging to a board is a CEO who may not be a great "public company CEO." The leader who successfully leads and motivates an early team of technology evangelists may not be best suited for managing public investors, pension funds, and regulatory constraints. There are only a handful of technology startup CEOs that successfully went on to manage their public companies. They include Bill Gates, Andy Grove, Michael Dell, and Scott McNeally. The complete list is not much longer.

Investment bankers play important roles in exits. Often an investment banker helps drive to either outcome, not necessarily knowing which way it will go. You should pick a partner in your investment bank who will help you maximize those returns by looking at both options. Often the only way to get a higher M&A value is to proceed with an IPO roadmap, and vice versa. You engage with as many buyers as you can to get a sense of what your valuation would be in the public market if you went public.

Selling a Company

Typically you engage with someone who will play an agency role in maximizing the value, like an investment banker, who creates an auction of the assets. He or she finds two or three buyers to compete for the company's assets – a kind of eBay of M&A.

Generally in this market good buyers are companies that care about the problems you are trying to solve. Most start-ups try to fulfill a need that a large player is not meeting. They can see on the radar screen what Microsoft, Intel, or Cisco is doing, and go on to discover an area they have not focused on. The entrepreneur sets out to solve this problem. Along the way the entrepreneur pays attention to what some of these big players are doing. In an ideal world the entrepreneur introduces a product about the time the big companies figure out they are missing it. You look to these big companies as potential buyers.

It is generally believed there is always a buyer, depending on the price. You have to keep a strong hand while you work with multiple bids. If a company needs a buyer but cannot find one, it may eventually disintegrate. Usually, however, a company can find a buyer – you just have to agree on price.

A company that cannot find a buyer has alternatives to bankruptcy. One such alternative is called an earn-out arrangement, in which an acquirer says, "I do not want to incur the risk and liability of buying these assets. I won't give you any money, but I will take you under my wing in a contractual relationship. I will pay your investors a percentage of the proceeds from this relationship." An earn-out arrangement is a conditional purchase.

If your company were forced to sell because there is no money, you would have to move into an asset sale, where you try to maximize scrap value. You are selling scrap metal – not a car. You do not want to get into this situation, but if you do, there is a market for scrap metal. You go to companies with which you've had fruitful relationships and see how much you can get for your assets. It's the same list of buyers you would go to in an M&A exit, but this time you are only offering them scrap.

Terms and Conditions of M&A Sales

When evaluating an offer for purchase of a venture-backed company, the following components are usually evaluated:

- Total consideration
- Stock or cash
- Stock price collars
- Employee option treatment
- Stock option acceleration and vesting
- Lockup agreement
- Employee agreement

The first point in a potential acquisition evaluation is the total price offered. Venture investors will seek a multiple on their invested cash as well as a good exit for their management teams. Five to ten times invested capital is considered a very successful exit for venture-backed companies. Clearly, only very capital efficient companies, (those which have built value on little cash) can benefit from a 5- 10X multiple in an environment where valuations are capped in the $100-$200M range.

The agreed upon consideration may be stated in cash, stock or a combination of both. Depending on the evaluation of the acquirer's stock, one or the other may be more favorable. If the stock is considered "good," say for example, Intel or Microsoft, investors will view it favorably. If it is not good, venture investors will prefer cash. The reason is simple: because of holding periods, the venture investors want to avoid losing the value of their exit during the holding period. Cash doesn't lose its value and a good stock is seen as having upside potential.

If any part of the transaction is done with stock, the company will want to negotiate a stock price collar or similar protection. A stock collar protects the seller (and the buyer) from future fluctuations in the price of the buyer's stock. Assume that BigCo makes a stock offer to purchase NewCo for $100M when its stock is trading at $10/share. It makes this offer with 100,000 shares of BigCo stock. Immediately after the announcement (but before the close), its stock drops to $8/share. Without some adjustment, the NewCo acquisition has suddenly dropped in value without any fault of its own. To prevent this volatility, buyers and sellers in stock transactions agree on a mechanism (stock collars are but one example) whereupon changes in stock price are reflected in a commensurate rachet in the deal structure.

Employee stock options must often be negotiated separately (or together) with the overall purchase. The value of employee stock ownership is sometimes (but not always) treated separately from the value of the ongoing concern. Savvy acquirers know that the real value of their acquisition is based on the people they acquire, not only the technology. As a result, they will often take over current stock option obligations and convert them to their companies' stock option structure. The objective again is to ensure long-term participation by key members of the management team

Venture board members often negotiate acceleration agreements for their management teams. These employee agreements specify a percentage of a manager's stock options that will immediate accelerate upon "change of control" (i.e., acquisition). This structure is often revisited during an M&A transaction. For reasons stated earlier, the acquirer typically has every incentive to retain management talent and will want to look through these prior agreements to ensure that talent doesn't float out the door the second the acquisition closes.

Lockup agreements for M&A activity are typically less onerous than IPOs but more negotiable. Depending on the relative size of the acquirer and acquiree, the acquirer may specify a lockup agreement for the sale of its stock. A typical number is six months, though it could range from less to several years. Again, venture investors may wish to calibrate the overall value of the deal on the lockup agreement. A very long lockup may take away the sparkle of the overall deal.

Finally, an acquirer may seek to sign employment agreements with key members of the management team. A savvy acquirer will not wait long to do this, once again understanding the value of ongoing employees. Here the venture board may play its strongest hand. Because it has built up long-term relationships with its management team, the board is best suited for helping negotiate differences. For example, a technical founder may refuse to sign up for a four-year agreement with the acquirer, citing the itch to go out and start a new company. This action might tank the overall deal. A board member may be needed to help "convince" the founder to sign, using both a carrot (without your signature we don't have a deal and that's the worst outcome for everybody) to a stick (if you don't sign, you'll never get venture funded again, why would anybody back you if you won't help them exit?). Typically a middle ground is found so that the deal may close.

The Exit Hierarchy

After an exit, in the process of "settling up," the creditors are paid first. The creditors are prioritized as senior and junior creditors. You must pay employee benefits first, then taxes if owed, then secured senior creditors, then unsecured creditors, like people with accounts receivable and lines of credit, and then, finally, the preferred and common equity holders. Preferred equity holders get paid first, then common shareholders.

If the purchase price is below the original value, the equity holders typically get nothing. The debtors must be paid first, and only after they are clear are the equity holders paid. If there is not enough money, the common shareholders and VCs usually receive no return.

Entrepreneurs' Mistakes

The most common mistake made by an entrepreneur is believing their company is worth more than it is. It is the same mistake a house seller makes, but in business, the value can go to zero in days.

Entrepreneurs generally think that what they built with their blood, sweat, and tears is worth more than someone is willing to pay for the company. Anything is worth only what someone is willing to pay for it. No other valuation matters. There is no intrinsic value where supply and demand meet. Entrepreneurs fail to recognize this fact. They further fail to recognize that value can drop as easily as it can rise.

In the bubble period, an entrepreneur who thought half a billion dollars was not enough for their company often led it into bankruptcy six months later. Today the same mentality survives, except that a zero or two have been removed. Entrepreneurs still do not recognize what their companies are actually worth.

This impasse causes problems because buyer and seller are not reasonably aligned on the value of the company and so cannot close the transaction. You have to bid and ask in terms of what you think your company is worth. Generally you do not have the latitude of being apart by ten times the offered price. If buyer and seller are not reasonably aligned on price, there will be no sale.

Golden Rules of Successful Exits

Successful exits depend largely on maintaining a continuing dialogue with potential buyers. You are always representing the company. Keep selling: Treat every meeting and every conversation as a potential liquidity step.

Remember the two-humped camel. Understand that valuation is often high in a concept stage, and then it goes through a valley of death before it comes back up in terms of profit. Entrepreneurs who fail to see the valley of death often die there.

Understand that exit valuation is only a function of what a buyer will pay. There is no other intrinsic value. Entrepreneurs are wrong to think their companies are worth more than someone is willing to pay.

Grasp the issue of timing. In the technology market, your company could be on top of the world one day and at the bottom the next. There are no guarantees of success for either a start-up or an established company. For start-ups that uncertainty is magnified a thousand times. Do not be cocky.

Bart Schachter is a Founding and Managing Partner of Blueprint Ventures. Bart brings 16 years of entrepreneurial, venture, and industry operating experience in communication semiconductors, wireless, and infrastructure software. He has a demonstrated track record of working with early stage venture-backed start-ups, having backed and served on the boards of over 25 emerging technology companies since 1996.

Bart's current investment focus includes wireless technologies, nanoelectronics, and communications semiconductors.

Bart started his venture capital career in late 1996 by investing in early stage companies while at Intel Capital where he was Director of Networking and Communication Investments. Creating an ecosystem investment strategy, Bart led investments spanning all areas of communications infrastructure including service providers, systems, and semiconductor companies. Bart's investments returned approximately a billion dollars in realized gains. He built a reputation for being a trusted partner to the management teams and boards of Covad Communications, Copper Mountain Networks, CopperCom, NorthPoint Communications, Media4, AccessLan, IteX, GlobeSpan, Broadband Technologies, and Broadcom.

Bart built his operating experience earlier in his eight-year tenure at Intel. Before becoming a venture capitalist, he held several senior operating roles within Intel's Networking and Communications Division. His product line responsibilities included network adapters and switches, storage area networking, network management software and video conferencing. As a General Manager, he was responsible for several product lines in the US and internationally, including the acquisition and integration of a network management start-up in Israel.

Before joining Intel, Bart was a successful entrepreneur, founding an enterprise LAN services and integration firm, later acquired by Alphanet, a $140 million national systems integration firm.

Bart holds a BS in Computer Engineering from Cornell University and an MBA from the Anderson Graduate School of Management at UCLA.

His current board responsibilities include BayPackets, Bermai, and KeyEye.

In his spare time, Bart enjoys mountain biking, playing tennis, running and traveling. He has lived throughout the world and is fluent in three languages.

Dedication: *To my partners George Hoyem, Ashley Read, and David Frankel.*

Achieving Liquidity from Venture Capital Investments

Dr. Robin Louis

President
Ventures West Management Inc.

Introduction

Venture capital investors commit funds to their portfolio companies with the expectation of earning high rates of return. The risky nature of venture investment dictates that the companies that do well must generate high returns because other companies in the portfolio will provide low or no returns at all. Most venture capital investments are made in companies that are private at the time the investment is first made. The investment becomes successful when the investor can recoup his initial investment and a profit; this only occurs when the investment becomes "liquid." Liquid means that the investor can exchange his ownership position in the company for cash. When an investor sells his stake in a company, he is said to have achieved an "exit."

Venture Capital Investing

Many venture capital investors, such as Ventures West, focus on investment in early stage companies. This means that, at the time of initial investment, the company may lack some or all of: a) products, b) customers, c) revenue and d) profits. It is this lack of demonstrated value in the product and lack of established track record that makes venture investing so risky. Building a new enterprise to create a new product, breaking into a new market, convincing initial customers to accept an untried product from a startup company, establishing the sales & service capability, and all the other things that starting a new enterprise requires, is a daunting task. This accounts for the focus which venture capital investors place on management teams. A good team can often overcome product, market, and competitive barriers to build a valuable new company while an incomplete or poorly functioning team will often cause a good product/market opportunity to be lost.

Starting at an early stage, the time required to get a company to liquidity is usually substantial. While there are ways to achieve early exits as described below, the time to build a company from a startup to a leading company in a substantial market is usually more than five years. A company needs time to develop and test its product, introduce it to the market, obtain initial customers, make the product well known in its marketplace, build a sales force and sales channels, develop a substantial customer base and thereby generate substantial revenues and profits. At Ventures West, our focus is on making our first investment when the company is at the startup stage and then helping build an enterprise with long-term value. Our expected investment timeline is four to eight years (the expected time to exit) and there have been cases where we were shareholders for much longer.

Two obvious factors that affect investment timelines are: a) how quickly the company grows its business and b) how quickly potential acquirers or the public markets recognize the company's success. Ventures West's investment strategy is to invest in sectors that have good long-term fundamental product value and market dynamics and to focus on helping the company achieve its key business milestones. If the entrepreneur, together with his management team and his investors, is able to build a market leading enterprise, and if the company is in an attractive sector, then the acquirers and/or public markets will eventually recognize the value and provide the exit. However, this is not left to chance—there are many things that can and should be done to plan for the eventual exit, to increase the probability that the exit will happen, and to increase the value at the time of exit.

One key factor in achieving a successful exit is market leadership. The best exits occur when a company has the best technology, the best market penetration, the best brand, the best customer list, the largest revenue and the highest profitability of all the companies in that particular business. Our experience is that there is always a premium attached to the market leading company. Market leadership will improve both the probability of a liquidity event and the value of the company when liquidity is achieved.

Types of Liquidity Events

There are two fundamental types of liquidity events—a sale of the company and an initial public offering ("IPO"). The right exit strategy depends primarily on the company and the industry in which it operates. A company in a broad market space that can grow to be quite large may be an IPO candidate. Companies focused on narrower product or market niches, or with products that ought to be part of something larger, are more likely to obtain liquidity by strategic sale.

Management teams often focus on an IPO because it is viewed as the ultimate validation of the company's success. Also, the company remains independent and has the "glamour" of being a public company. The IPO provides substantial cash resources and also publicly traded stock that can be used as currency for acquisitions—so the IPO substantially expands the company's ability to build its business.

If a company is acquired, it usually becomes a subsidiary or unit of a larger entity, and therefore loses its independence. After an acquisition, the acquired company may be merged with the acquirer, offices may be consolidated and staffing may be reduced so that this has a negative impact on employees. In other cases, the acquiring company uses the acquisition to build a new division, provides additional resources and opportunities for the staff are expanded thus allowing the acquired company to develop to a position that it never could have achieved on its own.

For venture capital investors, exit by strategic sale is the more frequent route to liquidity. In the U.S. from 1998 to 2003, 77 percent of liquidity events for venture-backed companies were strategic sales while only 23 percent were IPOs.

Strategic or Trade Sales

The sale of a company occurs when a buyer (the "acquiring company" or "acquirer") and the company to be bought (the "target company") agree on a price and the target company is sold to the acquirer. This is typically called a "strategic sale" or "trade sale."

Strategic sale—strategic rationale
There are many potential motivations for trade sales. The acquirer may want:

- *Technology*—the acquirer will generally want to incorporate the technology into its product line, as with the recent acquisition of OctigaBay Systems Corp. by Cray Inc. OctigaBay is developing a low-latency, self-monitoring, self-healing, high performance computer based on an innovative architecture. The product could ultimately deliver the same computer power as a high performance computer but at a fraction of the cost. By acquiring OctigaBay, Cray extends its product portfolio and increases its addressable market, including entry to mid-level high performance computing companies. The acquisition occurred when OctigaBay had prototypes operating in its laboratory but the company had not made any sales—Cray wanted the technology as they had the distribution channels that they believe can successfully drive the products into the market.

- *Market presence*—the acquirer wants to obtain an established position in a market or eliminate competition, as with the

Standard Register acquisition of InSystems Technologies. InSystems is a provider of insurance portal software and document automation solutions to insurance companies. Standard Register, a document-management company, acquired InSystems in order to access new markets and to provide complementary products to their customers. Standard Register, which focuses on banking, healthcare and other markets, expanded its reach into the insurance industry by acquiring an established player in that sector.

- *Revenues and profits; market share increase*—the acquirer may simply want to increase the size of its business and its market share. Hydrogenics Corp. acquired Greenlight Power, a global supplier of testing and diagnostic equipment to the fuel cell industry, in January 2003. Greenlight had supplied fuel cell test equipment to the world's premier fuel cell stack manufacturers, component manufacturers, system integrators and research organizations. The acquisition pooled the resources of both companies and nearly doubled the size of this core element of Hydrogenics´ business and made Hydrogenics the dominant company in this sector. This acquisition also brought new technology to Hydrogenics.

- *Product completion*—the acquirer may have a product that is complementary to the products of the target company so that the combined product provides a more complete solution for the end customers. Research in Motion acquired Plazmic Inc. to get access to that company's technology for implementing Java based applications on handheld devices. RIM has recently released a new line of devices that incorporate this technology. This is a clear example of acquiring a technology in order to accelerate product development.

These examples are from Ventures West's portfolio and every venture capital investor will have many similar examples of purchases of their investments for strategic reasons.

Strategic sale—financial structure

From a financial structure point of view, there are two main types of acquisition—purchase of shares and purchase of assets.

In an acquisition by way of acquisition of shares, the acquirer makes an offer to the shareholders of the target company to purchase (usually all and not less than all of) the shares of the target company. This way, the target company stays intact with basically a new 100 percent shareholder. There are many benefits to this form of transaction: (a) it is much easier to formally transfer shares of a company than it is to transfer a large number of assets (and some assets such as customer contracts may be difficult to transfer); (b) there are usually no third party consents required under a sale of shares whereas a sale of assets usually require consents from licensees, licensors, and possibly from other suppliers; (c) sale of shares does not trigger sales tax liability to the acquirer; (d) the acquirer sometimes receives the benefit of tax losses which have been realized by the target company and may result in additional consideration that the acquirer is prepared to pay to the selling shareholders; and (e) the selling shareholders may have better tax results from a sale of shares as capital gains may be realized and certain other tax exemptions and deferrals may be taken advantage of. A purchase of shares may be structured so that capital gains taxes are deferred until the time that the selling shareholder ultimately sells the shares of the acquirer (if shares were the form of consideration received by the selling shareholder under the transaction). One of the disadvantages to the acquirer in a share transaction is that the acquirer does not get a "bump" (increase) in the tax cost of the underlying assets and may lose a portion of the depreciation deductions otherwise available under an asset transaction. A major consideration for the acquiring company is that if shares in the target company are acquired, the acquirer is taking on all of the liabilities of the target company and so extensive due diligence will be required to ensure that these are well understood.

If the acquisition is structured as a purchase of assets, the acquirer makes an offer for the assets of the target company rather than acquiring the legal entity that is the target company. This way, the target company and the acquirer can agree to transfer only selected assets rather than selling all assets. This may allow the target company to realize value from some assets that are not desired by the acquiring company or continue the business utilizing those unwanted assets. Under this purchase of asset scenario, the proceeds from the sale of the selected assets will be received by the target company (not the shareholders) and then must be distributed to the stakeholders of the target company, including the creditors. Sometimes this distribution becomes complicated as taxes may be due and payable by the target company and, in all cases under the sale of asset scenario, it will require continued administration to process this distribution. One major benefit to the acquiring company of an acquisition of assets is that the assets and liabilities are spelled out in the legal documents and therefore the risk of taking on unknown liabilities is less than in the case of acquisition of shares.

Strategic sale—types of payment
There are three basic ways in which the acquiring company pays for its acquisition: a) cash; b) assumption of debt; and c) stock of the acquiring company. Payment may be entirely in one form, or a mixture.

Cash and assumption of debt are forms of consideration that are very simple to understand. Stock of the acquiring company on the other hand requires much more analysis and examination of: (a) the level of liquidity for the stock (i.e. can the stock of the acquiring company be sold—is there a market for the stock and do the regulatory rules permit such sale); (b) the value of the stock now and the expected value of the stock when the selling shareholder can or desires to sell the stock; (c) the legal rights and obligations as a shareholder of the acquiring company; and (d) the tax consequences of receiving the stock (the tax on the sale of shares may in some cases be deferred until the ultimate sale of stock of the acquiring company).

Under a sale of either shares or assets, the acquirer often will require that a portion of the proceeds be held in escrow for a certain period of time to provide security for breaches of representations and warranties provided to the acquirer. This is commonly called an "escrow holdback." The terms and conditions of such escrow holdback are usually "hotly" negotiated items during the sale process and considerations include provisions such as: a) the amount of the escrow; b) the time period for the escrow; c) how the escrow is to be split among the various stakeholders of the target company; d) the terms under which the escrow can be reclaimed by the acquirer because the representations and warranties have been breached; and e) who actually holds the escrow assets. This escrow holdback is usually more complicated when the transaction consideration is in the form of stock of the acquiring company rather than cash or assumption of debt.

Strategic sale—planning in advance
If the company does not expect to grow to a size where an IPO is possible, or if it is in a specialized business where it appears that the company's product needs to be part of a broader product line, then a strategic sale will generally be the expected liquidity event.

The company's board and management should think, early in the company's life, about the product, competitive, and marketplace factors that will drive or limit the future sale alternatives. It is critical to understand the universe of potential acquirers and potential acquisition candidates. You do not want to have all the potential buyers satisfy their needs by purchasing your competitors!

Once the competitive and acquisition landscape has been defined, the company needs to consider these strategic issues as it develops its business. For example, if a company is selling product through indirect channels, it is often the case that a channel partner is a potential acquirer. Alliances should be built with this in mind. Similar issues arise in product bundling, technology licensing, co-operative sales efforts and other aspects of a company's business.

In order to create opportunities for a future strategic sale, there is a delicate balance that must be maintained when building business alliances. On the one hand, the company wants to leverage business partners as much as possible to build its business. On the other hand, the company must not become so dependant on one business partner that that partner is the only potential acquirer. This would be the case, for example, if a large part of a company's business was sourced through one channel partner. In that case, the business might have little value if acquired by anyone other than that channel partner, especially if the acquisition by another party would cause these sales to stop. When the only potential buyer will be the channel partner, as in this example, the purchase price will be low.

A good buyer is one that can combine the acquired company with its own business and achieve an array of benefits. For example, if the acquiring company has a large customer base and is about to acquire a company with a product that can be sold to those customers, the acquisition would be quite valuable. In fact, this type of situation can make the acquired company more valuable to the acquirer than it is by itself. The best acquirers are those that have an opportunity to reap substantial value—a transaction where "one plus one equals three."

After determining the types of companies that are potential buyers, a company looking to be acquired should think about what characteristics would make it attractive to an acquirer. The characteristics that matter generally relate to product, market share, customer list, distribution channels and financial performance. Several of these have been discussed above in the context of what makes a company an attractive acquisition candidate. Financial parameters are also important. Acquirers are often public companies and are very sensitive to the impact of the acquisition on their financial performance, from several perspectives. First, an acquirer will be reluctant to reduce its earnings by acquiring a company that is losing money, unless cost and revenue synergies offer the prospect of creating net new profit once the acquired company is merged into the acquirer. Second, the acquiring company will be sensitive to the diluting effect on its earnings per share of stock issued for the acquisition. Third, as the public markets like consistency and predictability, the acquiring company will be sensitive to any increase in revenue or earnings volatility that the acquisition may bring.

Finally, it is essential to think about the potential for strategic sale when a company is raising money from a shareholder (the "strategic shareholder") who has an interest in the company that is other than purely financial. The motives for strategic shareholders to invest in the company are generally focused on business objectives other than rate of return and therefore they are quite different from financial investors. This would be the case, for example, if a potential strategic shareholder is a business partner or has an interest in the technology, distribution channels, customers, or any other aspect of the business. The risk is that the strategic shareholder may not want the company to be sold in a transaction that financially attractive, because of the strategic shareholder's other interests in the company. For example, this might occur if a software company had a business relationship with a systems integrator and the systems integrator was also a shareholder. If a different systems integrator made an offer to purchase the company, the systems integrator that is the business partner may see this as potentially ending their business relationship with the target company and so might try to block the sale. It is imperative that any such strategic shareholders only be allowed to make an investment in the target company in a way that prohibits the strategic shareholder from stopping the sale of the company. Typically the way such a strategic shareholder would block a sale would be to vote their shares against the acquisition. If the strategic shareholder held enough shares, they could prevent the sale. One way to overcome this potential problem is to include a "drag along" provision in the target company's articles of incorporation or in a contract amongst the shareholders. This provides that, if a specified percentage of the target company's shareholders vote to approve a transaction, that all other shareholders are forced to participate in the transaction—in the example described above, the strategic investor would be "dragged along," i.e. forced to participate in the transaction.

Strategic sale—mechanics

The acquisition process is generally initiated by one of four types of events. First, the company may be approached by a prospective acquirer. Second, it may become evident to the company's management and board that consolidation in the marketplace is starting, or about to start, and the company should be proactive rather than waiting for acquirers to approach the company. Third, the company may find itself in an advantageous market share, technology, competitive or brand position that may deteriorate in the future—and therefore may want to capitalize on its current situation. Fourth, customers may be demanding a broader suite of products and therefore are, in effect, suggesting a business combination.

Once the process has started, there are two types of approaches.

- *Single acquirer*—in the case where an acquirer has approached the company with an offer to purchase, or if there is one prime acquirer candidate, the company may decide to talk to only that one potential buyer. The company may decide to do this by itself or it may hire a merger and acquisition specialist (generally an investment banker) to assist with the process.

- *Multiple acquirers*—if the company believes that there are multiple potential acquirers then it will undertake a process to try to interest a number of parties in making the acquisition.

Hiring an investment banker for the purpose of assisting in a merger and acquisition ("M&A") transaction is similar in many ways to hiring an investment banker for an IPO, except that in this case he will be an M&A specialist. The selection criteria for an investment banker in this situation include the following:

- *Industry knowledge*—it is critical that the banker understand the industry in which the company being sold operates, the major players in this industry and the synergies with other companies—this allows them to create a complete list of potential buyers.

- *M&A experience*—this is a specialized activity where experience in several prior transactions is invaluable.

- *Not too busy*—in times of high M&A activity, the investment bankers become very busy. You want to have the attention of the senior people in the organization who are managing the process.

The process that takes place to affect the sale will generally include the following steps:

- *Decision*—the company decides to sell itself and to hire an investment banker to assist in this.

- *Contact investment bankers*—the company determines which investment bankers have relevant experience and may be willing and able to take on the assignment.

- *"Bake off" or "beauty contest"*—a selected group of investment bankers (generally about three) will be invited to present their credentials and experience.

- *Investment banker selection*—the board selects the investment banker.

- *Due diligence*—the investment banker conducts due diligence to ensure that the selling company is as represented.

- *Prepare book*—the investment banker together with company management prepare a book which describes all aspects of the company's products, markets, operations and future potential.

- *Define list of potential contacts*—this is the list of potential buyers to be contacted. There may be priority groupings and there may be potential buyers who will not be contacted because of potential adverse market impact.

- *Initial contact*—the investment banker contacts the potential buyers, ascertains their interest and, if appropriate, has them sign non-disclosure agreements and then provides the book.

- *Follow-up*—the investment banker will determine which potential buyers are interested in pursuing a transaction after having reviewed the book.

- *Due diligence*—a small number of potential acquirers will perform due diligence to learn more about the company they propose to acquire, and ensure that it is as represented in the book. This generally will be an extensive process which will include visiting the target company, meeting key management, examining all financial and legal records of the target company (which may be collected in a "data room"), customer calls, analysis of product, intellectual property audit, and examination of all contracts. This is an arduous process and one which will give the potential acquirer deep knowledge of the target company's products, business and customers.

- *Offers*—the investment banker will organize offers. Ideally the buyers will be forced into a defined schedule for making initial offers and subsequent improvements of the proposed terms if an auction can be instigated.

- *Selection*—the company's board and management select one preferred bidder.

- *Negotiation*—definitive terms are negotiated with the acquirer.

- *Announcement*—the transaction is announced.

- *Completion of due diligence*—the acquiring company completes its due diligence on the target company.

- *Final documentation*—the final documentation of the deal is completed.

- *Regulatory approvals*—any necessary regulatory approvals are obtained.

- *Closing*—the transaction closes—documents are signed and payment is made.

Initial Public Offering (IPO)

An IPO or "going public" is the selling of shares in a company to the public and listing of the company's shares on a stock exchange. A company whose shares do not trade on a stock exchange is referred to as a "private company" and after the IPO, the shares trade on an exchange and the company is referred to as a "public company." After the IPO, the shareholders who have invested in the company when it was private can obtain liquidity by selling their shares in the public markets.

The IPO event achieves two main goals—the company raises capital from the new shares sold and the shares owned by the investors prior to the IPO are transformed from illiquid shares in a private company to liquid shares that trade on a stock exchange and thus can readily be sold for cash.

The gating factor, which determines if a company can go public, is the receptivity of the public markets. When the public markets will accept companies with certain characteristics, it is said that "the IPO window is open" for these companies. The public markets are very fickle in their acceptance of IPOs, particularly for young companies. The graph below shows the number of venture-backed IPOs on the NASDAQ—clearly there is great variability in the total number of IPOs in each year and also in the receptivity of the public markets to different industry sectors.

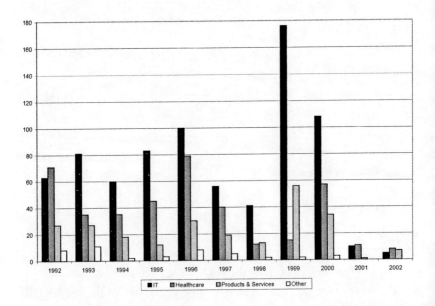

The public markets demand different characteristics from different types of companies in order to allow an IPO. For example, software companies typically require: a) $10–20 million in quarterly revenue; b) good growth, both demonstrated in the past and prospectively; and c) one or two quarters of profitability. In "hot" markets, the revenue requirement may be reduced and the profitability requirement may be relaxed to require that the company just be close to profitability. Biotechnology companies, on the other hand, require a very different set of characteristics. Therapeutics companies typically require: a) a product candidate in phase II clinical testing; b) one or two other products in the pipeline that are close to, or in, clinical testing; and c) two or more years of cash in the bank. In "hot" markets, a "platform" company, one with a unique technology but no specific product candidates, may be an IPO candidate.

However, achieving the characteristics described above does not guarantee that an IPO will be possible. The markets go through periods when IPOs can be sold—"IPO window open"—and others when the IPO window is closed—even for companies with similar characteristics. The determining factor is the appetite of the buyers of the shares that the company proposes to issue. There are two main types of buyers—institutional buyers such as mutual funds, pension funds and other professional money managers, and individual investors. If these buyers are willing to purchase the newly issued stock, and it appears that there will be interest in purchasing the company's stock once the IPO has happened (and the stock is trading on a stock exchange), then the IPO can proceed. The appetite of these investors does vary widely. During the Internet boom of 1998-2000, the market accepted IPOs of companies that did not meet the characteristics described above and, in many cases, had no substantial revenues at all. Conversely, during 2001 and 2002, markets in North America would accept IPOs of only very large and established companies. The graph on page 146 shows this very clearly. There were a total of 249 venture-backed IPOs on the NASDAQ in 1999 but only 20 in 2002.

It is very difficult, or perhaps impossible, to predict when the IPO window will open and close. The venture investor must therefore make his initial commitment to a company without any assurance that an IPO will be possible at any particular time. The best strategy therefore is to focus on building a company that can take advantage of the opportunity when the IPO window opens.

Initial Public Offering—mechanics

An IPO is the right course of action for a company if: a) the IPO window is open for the company; b) the company wants to become a public company; c) the company has "use of proceeds," i.e. has good use for the money to be raised by the sale of the new shares to be issued and d) the company is able to find an investment banker to manager the IPO process. Generally speaking, an investment banker will be available if the new issue (the new shares to be issued) can be sold—so it is really the receptivity of the buyers of the stock who determine if an IPO will be possible.

The investment banker is sometimes referred to as an "underwriter." This term arises from one form of IPO transaction (an "underwritten deal") where the investment banker commits to purchase a specified number of newly issued shares at a specified price. The investment banker bears the risk that he will be able to sell the shares. Underwritten deals are generally only possible for large companies with long stable track records. The other type of IPO is a "best efforts" transaction where the IPO process is undertaken without any guarantee that it will be completed. If at the end of the process sufficient buyers cannot be found, then the IPO will fail—the new shares will not be sold and the company's stock will not be listed on a public stock exchange. For venture-backed companies, particularly in the technology sector, IPOs are generally undertaken on a best efforts basis.

One of the key factors in leading up to a successful IPO is choosing the right investment banking syndicate. This group will generally consist of a lead and two or three other investment bankers. The lead investment banker is key to a successful IPO. Unfortunately, there may not be a wide choice of investment bankers prepared to take the lead role in the IPO process. However, if there is a choice, the following criteria should be used to determine which banker should be the lead. The ideal banker should have: (a) led prior IPOs in the same or similar business as the company making the IPO; (b) a high quality, experienced, senior team committed to the IPO; (c) existing relationships with institutions which are likely buyers of the stock; and (d) a moderate level of other deals the investment banker is working on so as not to distract the company's IPO process.

The IPO process is quite well established and requires a huge amount of effort by the senior management team. This will be an all-consuming event for the CEO, the CFO, and others in the company for several months. The process will also entail spending a significant amount of money on legal fees and travel costs without knowing whether the IPO will be completed. The process generally includes the following steps:

- *Decision*—The company's board decides that the IPO is the right course and if necessary discusses the decision to proceed with the IPO with major shareholders.

- *Find investment bankers*—the company solicits interest from a select list of investment bankers.

- *"Bake off" or "beauty contest"*—a selected group of investment bankers present and market themselves to the company's board so that the board can select the syndicate of investment bankers and the lead underwriter.

- *Due diligence*—the investment bankers complete a process of due diligence on the company to gain familiarity with the business and prospects of the company and determine the likelihood of a successful IPO.

- *Determine target size of issue*—Management and the investment bankers determine and agree on the planned number of shares to be sold in the IPO, the exchange on which the company's shares will trade and whether the IPO will be 100 percent treasury shares or whether some portion will be in the form of existing shares being sold to the public (called a "secondary"). The number of shares to be sold in an IPO is typically in the range of 20 percent to 30 percent of the company and is determined based on: a) the fraction of the company that the board is willing to sell; b) the amount of money for which the company has good uses; and c) the amount of stock that the investment banker believes can be sold.

- *Draft prospectus*—the investment bankers, with the assistance of management of the company, lawyers and accountants, draft a prospectus.

- *Obtain approval*—the draft prospectus is submitted to the securities regulators. At this point, the fact that the company is attempting an IPO becomes public information and in the US, the prospectus also generally becomes public. There is a back and forth process involving the company and the securities regulators where the regulators make comments and the company revises the prospectus to respond. Hopefully, the result is an approved prospectus. At this point, the company and the investment bankers may market the IPO to the public.

- *Marketing*—with the assistance of the investment bankers, management of the company visits institutional investors and other brokers to market the issue, i.e. to solicit their interest in purchasing stock in the company as part of the IPO transaction. This is called the "road show." After the completion of all marketing, the investment bankers create a "book" of subscribers—those parties that are prepared to subscribe for stock under the public offering.

- *Pricing*—the investment banker and the company determine the price at which the stock will be sold. This is determined based on the investment banker's assessment of the sensitivity of the buyers to price—the trick is to sell the stock at the highest price possible which: a) will allow the desired number of shares to be sold (there are sufficient buyers at this price) and b) has the prospect of the public market price of the stock, once it starts trading, being moderately higher than the IPO price so that the IPO buyers will be happy. The process of fixing the price at which the shares will be sold is known as "pricing" the IPO.

- *Completion*—the IPO is then completed—the investors acquire the shares as allocated by the investment banker, the company receives the funds from the issuance of the treasury shares, the selling shareholders receive the funds from the sale of the secondary shares (if any) and all shares of the company begin trading on the selected stock exchange.

Initial Public Offering—planning in advance

There are three issues that should be considered at the time that a company takes private investment capital, that relate to the potential of an eventual IPO:

- *Forced conversion*—the company should ensure that it can cause all classes of shares to be converted into common shares in the event of an IPO. This is required because a company must typically have only common shares when it goes public. Venture investors may resist a provision which allows their preferred shares to be converted to common since this takes away all of the special rights attached to the preferred shares however the investor will generally not resist if the IPO is going to provide good liquidity and is at a good price. Therefore, the venture investor will often require that the conversion can be forced only for a "Qualifying IPO" which is defined as one that is on a specified stock exchange, raises more than a threshold amount of money, and is priced above a threshold price. In this way, the venture investor has comfort that, if conversion is forced, there will be liquidity for the common shares.

- *Registration rights*—investors, particularly in the U.S., often require a registration rights agreement that allows the investor to require the company to make an IPO in specified circumstances and ensures that the investors shares are qualified for sale ("registered") as a part of any such IPO. In practice, an IPO will only be possible if the markets are receptive and so it is usually not possible for the investor to force this.

- *Management and discipline for the public markets*—a company that is expecting to become a public company at some time in the future needs to build its management team and develop its internal processes with this in mind.

Valuation

The decision to pursue an IPO or strategic sale is usually heavily influenced by the expected pricing of the transaction. Unfortunately, in both IPOs and strategic sales the price is not set until the end of the process. In the case of an IPO, the price is only fixed after the road show is completed and the investment banker has determined the level of interest and price sensitivity of the prospective buyers. In the case of strategic sale, the price is not fully known until the transaction is negotiated with the prospective purchaser.

There are however several ways in which prices can be estimated before the start of the process.

- *Public comparables*—the trading prices of comparable companies can be ascertained and can provide a guide as to the eventual valuation of the company to be sold.

- *Comparable transactions*—there may have been acquisitions of similar companies where the sale parameters have been disclosed in press releases, in public filings or in notes to financial statements. Also, several data gathering organizations track these types of transactions.

- *Comparable metrics*—metrics such as price/sales ratios and price/earnings ratios can be used to estimate value for companies in the same industry, even if they are not in the same marketplace.

- *Ability to pay*—it is often useful to calculate what a purchaser could pay and still have the transaction make a positive impact on its financial performance. Hopefully, the acquirer can pay a price much higher than that calculated by the metrics described above because they can generate improved financial results due to product, market, customer or other synergies. It is because of this that it is crucial to understand the motivation of the buyer and to estimate the impact of the acquisition on the buyer's business.

In all of these valuation calculations, factors such as size of the company (revenues, staff), market share and position, growth rate, profitability, technology and product strengths, distribution channels, and everything else that is critical to the business are considered. Estimating the value that may be achieved is one of the key tasks of an investment banker. However, it is important to realize that the estimate provided by the banker is just an estimate—there must be an understanding that the price will not be known until the end of the process. It is also important to understand the motivation of the investment banker—they are paid by way of commission on transactions that complete. Therefore, the natural tendency of an investment banker is to estimate a high price at the start of the process and get the company started on the sale process. At the end of the process, hopefully the originally estimated price will be realized. However, if it is not, the selling company may, in effect, be forced to sell because of the effort that has been expended or because of the impact of the sale process in the marketplace. From an investment banker's perspective this may be an acceptable result as they will receive their (reduced) commission. However, it may not be optimal for the selling company.

The Liquidity Event and Achieving Liquidity

It may seem that once the liquidity event has occurred the shareholders of the acquiring company will have either cash or stock of the acquiring company (or a combination of both) and that they will have achieved liquidity. However, this is often not the case.

Restrictions on sale of shares after an IPO
Once the IPO has happened and the stock is trading, there is a public market in which shares can be bought and sold. However, there are typically restrictions that apply to shares that were issued while the company was private (prior to the IPO).

- First, there is usually a 180-day lockup for employees of the company and for major shareholders of the company, including the venture investors. The underwriter does not want to see a flood of stock hitting the market and driving the price down immediately after the completion of the IPO. By locking up major shareholders at the outset, the underwriter can prevent this problem. After the 180-day lockout is over, the venture groups are free to sell their stocks. They may sell immediately or hold onto the stock in anticipation of a rise in stock price. Another option venture groups often take for liquid public securities is to distribute stock to their investors—pension funds and institutions—and give these entities the choice of selling it themselves or keeping it for the long term.

- Second, the sale of shares held by some shareholders will be restricted by securities regulations such as SEC Rule 144 and Rule 145. The applicability of these restrictions will depend on when the shares were purchased, the size of the shareholding and the price paid for the shares.

For management, there is an additional problem related to selling shares. The public markets do not look fondly on management selling large portions of their holding in the company they are managing. The public markets would question why management is bailing out of their own company after the management has, during the road show, described all of the advantages of owning shares in the company. While it may be legally permissible for management to sell their shares immediately after the lockout expires, doing so creates the appearance that management has no confidence in the company.

Allocating the proceeds of a strategic sale

Allocating the proceeds of a sale can be complicated. If a company has debt, the lenders typically have the right to be repaid first. Venture investors may have the next right to a portion of the proceeds if they invested in the company by way of preferred shares that have a liquidation preference. A "liquidation preference" is a provision that is negotiated at the time of investment that requires the company to pay a defined amount of money to the preferred shareholders, upon the happening of certain types of events, typically including the sale of the company. The effect of this is usually that the preferred shareholders get their money back before the common shareholders do. The common shareholders are last in line, and the options on common shares, which typically are held by management, are settled as a part of the common share payout.

There are numerous variations to this scenario. Preferred shares are usually convertible into common shares. If the price is high enough, the preferred shareholders will elect to convert their shares into common shares and take the payout as common shareholders.

In theory, if the purchase price is less than the liquidation preference, the entire purchase price goes to pay out whatever portion of the liquidation preference it can cover, and the common shareholders get nothing. In practice, the deal often doesn't turn out that way because the common shareholders usually include the key members of management by way of stock options, or because they hold founder's shares. If the management team is a key part of the acquisition, they will usually get some portion of the proceeds, if they are supportive of the transaction. Typically, each class of shareholders must approve the transaction. As a class, the common shareholders won't approve it unless they get some payout. Often this results in a negotiated division of the proceeds.

When to Try to Obtain Liquidity?

The question of when it is best to try to achieve liquidity is difficult to answer. Generally, at any time in a company's life it is critical to be focused on building the company, but also to be aware of the dynamics of the marketplace so that an opportune time for IPO or acquisition is not missed.

The key is to be ready to sell when these liquidity options become available. However, you do not want to sell:

- *Too early*—before the technology is proven, before the value proposition has been demonstrated, before there is customer validation or before you have achieved substantial market share; or

- *Too late*—when all the prospective acquirers have purchased a company in this industry, when the market is mature or declining, or when the technology and product have been eclipsed by new developments.

You do not want to try to make an IPO when the markets are weak and you do not want to try to sell when selling is your only option. You don't ever want your company to be in a situation where you have to sell because you are running out of cash—you want to sell when the company has some cash left. That situation allows you to say to potential buyers, "we don't really have to sell, but for all these strategic reasons that are good for us and good for you, it may be the best time for us to come together." Entrepreneurs tend to be optimistic—that quality is required of an entrepreneur—so they often expect that sales will come in more quickly than they actually do. If sales fall short of expectations, and the company finds itself in a cash bind, that will likely minimize the value that the shareholders obtain upon sale.

Early Exits

While profitable exits often require that the company be built to a substantial size and market position, this is not always the case. Where an acquiring company is seeking technology or the ability to enhance a product line, it may be possible to sell a company long before the company achieves a substantial penetration of the market. It is for this reason that early stage companies should be aware of the activities of potential acquirers. The buyer may be ready before the startup company is, but companies often have to take these opportunities when they present themselves, not when most convenient.

The Role of Venture Capitalists in Exits

Venture partners typically are very involved with creating, growing, and achieving liquidity in their portfolio companies. Many venture investors manage pools of funds that have defined lifetimes (usually ten years) and so the venture capitalist has a responsibility to his investors to ensure the portfolio is liquid by the end of the lifetime of the fund. Liquidity will generally not be forced by a venture investor, however, prospects for liquidity within the term of the fund will be one of the considerations when initially making the investment. Similarly, an entrepreneur should understand the investor's liquidity expectations before accepting an investment. It is important that the investor and the entrepreneur have similar views on liquidity. This includes timing, what the company should look like at the time of liquidity, and the potential liquidity options. One of the principal roles for the venture investor is to provide his experience and contacts with investment bankers and to help the company plan strategically for exit opportunities.

If a company can make an IPO, this is usually a happy event for all shareholders and for management and so all interests are aligned. However, this is not always the case for strategic sales. An acquiring company often sees the management team of the acquired as one of the principal assets being purchased and therefore they will want to make sure that the terms of the purchase leave the management team "happy." On the other hand, the acquirer will generally have no ongoing relationship with the non-management shareholders, which generally includes the venture investors. So, the buyer is strongly motivated to focus the transaction on the management shareholders. Venture investors should therefore participate in the sale negotiations, to ensure that the interests of all parties are protected.

Strategies for a Failing Company

The discussion above assumes that the company contemplating IPO or strategic sale is doing well and has attractive liquidity options. Unfortunately this is not always the case. What are the options if the company is not growing rapidly, is not achieving market leadership, does not have a growing and valuable customer base and generally is unlikely to be able to achieve a successful exit? Venture investors generally make initial investments in a company with the expectation that they will participate in subsequent financings ("follow-on investment rounds"). Follow-on investments will be made only if justified by the company's progress and its prospects at the time that the follow-on round is required. When a venture investor looks at a follow-on investment, he generally will look at the company as if it is a brand new opportunity that has just walked in the door, without prior involvement. A previous commitment of capital that has not worked out well is not a good reason to make a follow-on investment. It will be difficult or impossible for a venture-backed company to raise financing from new investors if the previous investors are not supportive. A common understanding of the financing strategy and prospects amongst the venture investors and the company management is key. If the prospects for a successful liquidity event are not good and the venture investors are not willing to provide follow-on financings, then there has to be an alternate plan. Both the venture investor and company management will want to develop a strategy that salvages the most value possible.

Every situation is different yet there are a few general rules but you must give yourself time to take action. Running out of cash is generally fatal and has a major negative impact on the value that is achieved. Therefore, for businesses that are not going well, action needs to be taken before the cash situation is critical—so that there is time to:

- *Reorient the business*—it may be possible to change the way that the company uses its core resources to give it a chance to try to build the business in a new way.

- *Sell the business*—as described above this can be a lengthy process.

- *Sell part of the business*—if the whole business cannot be sold as one entity, parts of it may be saleable.

- *Close down and sell assets*—as a last resort, this may salvage some value.

It is very important to think through the process, including the downside possibilities. Action must be taken by the board of a company with a business that is not progressing well, continues to use cash, and does not have a realistic hope of either getting cash flow to break even with existing resources, or raising additional financing. In this situation, if selling the company is the best alternative, this needs to be instigated at a time when the company has enough cash to continue operating through what can be a long process. The time required to go through the types of steps listed above can easily exceed a year.

If a company is running out of cash and can't find a buyer, and there is no way to carry on the business, then the directors have an obligation to shut down the company and obtain whatever they can for the shareholders. The time at which the directors must stop the company's operations is before it completely runs out of money as the directors must not allow the company to incur obligations that it cannot meet—for example, purchases for which it cannot pay, payroll for time worked, holiday pay, and government remittances which the company has collected from the employees. The directors are personally liable for some of these if the company is unable to pay the amounts owed.

An orderly shutdown of the company typically entails terminating the employees, settling amounts owed, terminating arrangements with customers, terminating leases and selling the assets of the company.

Final Thoughts

Achieving a good liquidity event is a combination of hard work, understanding the marketplace, and good luck. Hard work is required to build the company into an entity that will be attractive to public markets or to strategic acquirers. A deep understanding of your marketplace, key players and the interplay of strategic relationships is required to build relationships and avoid traps so that your company will be attractive to a number of strategic acquirers. Good luck is needed for the IPO markets or the strategic acquirers to recognize the attractions of the marketplace and your company at a time that optimizes its value.

Dr. Robin Louis is the President of Ventures West, one of Canada's largest privately owned venture capital companies. Robin joined Ventures West in 1991 and currently oversees the operations of the firm and its investment funds, as well as being an active venture investor. His investment activities focus primarily on the software industry and past investments include success stories such as Pivotal Corporation, which grew to be one of the largest enterprise software companies in Canada with a market capitalization in excess of $1 billion.

Prior to joining Ventures West, Robin was the CEO of Columbia Computing Services Ltd., a provider of software used in K-12 schools for administrative data management. Under Robin's leadership, Columbia became the dominant company in its industry, was listed on the Toronto Stock Exchange, and subsequently was sold to a British acquirer.

Robin has served on the boards of several Ventures West portfolio companies and currently serves as a director of Chancery Software Ltd., INEA Corporation and MaestroCMS Inc., as well as Chair of the board of Fincentric Corp. Robin is the current President, and a director of the Canadian Venture Capital Association.

Robin earned a B.S. (Honors) and M.S. degree from the University of Victoria and a Ph.D. in physics from the University of British Columbia.

Acknowledgment: I would like to acknowledge the assistance of David McIntyre, Christine Ramsay and Howard Riback in the preparation of this chapter. They provided key parts of the content and valuable commentary and advice.

Selling a Company the Right Way

Charles E. Harris

Chairman & CEO

Harris & Harris Group, Inc.

When an Exit Strategy is the Right Strategy

The pursuit of an exit strategy can come about for any of the various reasons. A third party might make an unsolicited offer. A change in the capital markets may make new alternatives available. Investors may feel that they are no longer adding value and that the company is approaching peak value under their stewardship. Perhaps the company needs more capital or needs some kind of strategic alliance. My firm does not manage third-party assets – just our firm's own capital – so we can be patient investors if we think that the investee company needs more time. But sometimes venture capitalists managing an expiring partnership or other fund may need to liquidate their holdings. In other words, the precipitating factors for a sale can be external or internal and can come from competitors, investors, management, employees, or various constituencies looking for liquidity.

Ideally, however, the owners of a business should pursue an exit strategy when the business is reaching its potential under their ownership. (Interestingly, they probably made their investment when the original owner had the same motivation.) For example, if a company needs a level of marketing and distribution to maintain its competitive position that it cannot produce on its own, then it may be time to sell to another company with those capabilities. Or perhaps a company is faced with a massive capital investment, and it makes more sense to sell to a larger company that either has that equipment or that can more easily afford to purchase it.

An IPO may be appropriate for a company if it will give the company access to needed capital at a more reasonable cost or provide publicly traded stock as currency to attract and retain employees or to make acquisitions. For us, our North Star – the guiding factor that governs our decisions – is always to try to determine what will best help the company reach its realistic potential. A company should not go public simply

SELLING A COMPANY THE RIGHT WAY

because the investors want out; going public should occur only if it is right for the company.

The process of selling a company should begin with an assessment of which assets are most valuable to various third parties in various packages. You then determine whether it makes better sense to sell the company piecemeal or as one entity. It's important to factor in the transaction costs of various strategies. You want to sell in an orderly and efficient way, while remaining alert to unforeseen opportunities and difficulties. From a monetary standpoint, the worst time to sell is when the company is experiencing a negative situation, but we still try to be guided by what is best for the company. In our experience, that usually turns out to be best for the investors, too.

Of course, the particular economic goals and potential of each party to the transaction need to be considered. You need to gather and assess information in concert with the company and other investors, not unilaterally. Venture capitalists almost always invest in a company with the goal of making it a stand-alone, independent company. Initially, the plan may be for it to go public through an IPO. However, at some point in time, you may conclude that an IPO is not the best path for the company and that the company would be best served by joining up with another entity. Your motive in selling a company should be the same motive that you had for investing in it: to make a good return on your capital by helping the company realize its realistic potential.

Considerations When Selecting a Strategy

Speaking from the vantage point of a venture capitalist, there are three basic exit strategies: an initial public offering or IPO; selling a company to a third party in a merger or acquisition; and selling your interest in a company to the management of that company. If a company has a strong, motivated management team and good internal cash flow, the latter option can be viable and a true win-win for buyer and seller.

The best exit strategy for venture capitalists offers them their desired return on investment and also leaves the company in good hands and sound financial shape. Even after a venture capitalist sells out of a company, that company remains part of his legacy. How the company fared in the sale and how considerate the venture capital firm was of the other stakeholders affects a firm's reputation and how it is viewed as a future partner by other venture capital firms, entrepreneurs and lenders, as well as by research universities that may be asked to entrust their intellectual property. Of course, the venture capitalist has a fiduciary responsibility to his limited partners or shareholders, which necessitates thinking very hard about realizing a good return on each investment. At the same time, shareholders and partners also have an interest in doing well in future investments. So it is important to all stakeholders that the firm considers its reputation and does not make decisions based solely on making the absolute last dollar on an individual investment. The venture capital business is a long game.

A management team may have different priorities than a venture capitalist. Management may want to maintain ownership of the company to protect its jobs or because they have continued confidence in the company's future under its current ownership. The management team may want to take the company public to avoid working for anyone else by selling to another company. There is always the potential of a separation of interest between management and the venture capitalists. As in all human affairs, early and open communication about this potential separation of interests is the best policy.

Insensitivity to management's needs and interests will damage the VC firm's reputation. Word will get around, and entrepreneurs will be less eager to do business with a greedy firm in the future. Even if the venture capital firm has enough power to force management into a decision, it is far preferable to make exit decisions in concert with the management team.

Individual Roles

Venture capitalists usually have more experience selling companies than the management team. In addition to personal experience, venture capitalists typically have contacts that are very important to a sale, such as with lawyers, mergers and acquisitions intermediaries, or decision makers within the acquiring company. The venture capitalist should have a good idea of which intermediaries to trust – and how far.

Even though it is unusual for CEOs to stay on (or to stay on happily) after the sale of a company, because the acquiring company is often not receptive to the entrepreneurial spirit, the CEO's intimate knowledge of the company is highly important in executing a sale. In addition to the venture capitalist and the CEO, key company personnel and lenders and other equity stakeholders must be considered in any exit strategy.

After a company is acquired, arrangements may be made to keep key employees with the company so that the acquirer is getting its money worth. These employees must then sort out their new career opportunities within the larger entity. After a sale or IPO, the venture capitalists are usually not involved for long in the ongoing business. Most venture capital firms are organized as limited partnerships. After an IPO or sale of a company for stock in another entity, they often choose to distribute shares to their limited partners rather than sell them, but the limited partners typically sell their shares when they receive them.

The level of involvement after the sale or IPO is different for management and employees than for investors. When a company goes public, investors must wait a period of time – typically six months – before they can dispose of holdings because of the lockup period. During this time, the economic fate of the management and the investors remains similar. But even then, a separation of economic interest takes place, because stock options may be part of the deal, and both management and employees may be participating in those options. Once a company goes public, there is often – but not necessarily always – a gradual parting of ways between venture capitalists and management.

Timeline for an Exit

As early stage venture capitalists, we typically plan on a holding period of about seven years from our initial investment, although our average and median holding periods have been about half of that. The economy can significantly affect an investment timeline. In a vibrant, growing economy or a robust capital market, the timeline may be shorter because the environment offers more IPO and acquisition opportunities. Conversely, in a prolonged economic slump and a long bear market, the timeline tends to be longer.

Fledgling companies are exquisitely sensitive to economic fluctuations. When the economy is not growing, capital spending budgets for established companies are stagnant or being reduced. Thus, there usually is very limited opportunity for new capital goods companies to gain sales traction with big companies during recessions. Only when large established companies are increasing their capital spending budgets is there much business at the margin for new companies. That is why new companies have such pronounced sensitivity to the economy, with the resultant effect on investment timelines. Therefore, it is rarely good timing to sell fledgling companies during economic slumps when such companies are typically struggling.

IPO Exit

An IPO is the right exit strategy when any of the following situations occur: a company needs capital that can come only from the public market; an IPO offers the lowest cost of capital; or a company needs publicly traded stock for acquisitions or in order to set up the stock incentives needed to continue attracting and retaining highly talented people. Also, investors who were active when the company was in its fledgling stage may no longer want to be involved once the company is further along in its development and has a more active internal management team. A company that has reached this point can usually deal with the distractions of being a publicly held company without taking its eye off its customers and its business.

Negotiation with the underwriters usually determines, in large part, how much of a company to sell in an IPO. The underwriters offer their opinion as to how much stock needs to be sold in order to have a viable public market for the shares, taking into account that a company needs enough shares so that institutions are interested in buying the stock and the aftermarket is reasonably liquid. On the other hand, there may not be an appetite amongst investors for more than a certain dollar amount of a company's stock.

Above all, the issuing company needs to consider the use of proceeds. The amount of stock the company is selling for its own account, as opposed to the account of its investors, should be appropriate to the company's investment needs. If there are investors in the company who would like to sell shares in the offering, in some circumstances such a sale may actually benefit the deal by giving it critical mass. But if the extra shares raise the issuing company's cost of capital, the venture capitalist should not insist on being included in the IPO, even if the underwriters will permit it.

Instead, the venture capitalist should plan ahead and think about a secondary offering after the company goes public. If the company is selling enough shares to create a viable public market and satisfy its capital needs, and the venture capitalist is confident of the company's prospects, the venture capitalist should let the stock season in the expectation that it will go higher.

Underwriters have a strong negotiating hand in the valuation of the company's IPO. Underwriters are in a competitive business, so they are heavily influenced in their valuation by "comparables." If the company is in a well-established market in which there are many comparable companies, it is relatively easy to assess how the marketplace will value that company. If a company does not have direct competitors, the valuation process becomes more difficult and usually involves more negotiation with the underwriters. In that case, underwriters place more emphasis on general factors such as economic characteristics, sustainable competitive advantages, profit margins, return on equity, growth rate, and the business cycle.

Liquidation

The smaller the company, the market capitalization and the management team, the less management will be able to liquidate in an IPO or subsequently in follow-on offerings in the public market. For example, Bill Gates can sell a very substantial amount of Microsoft stock on a regular basis – and it has almost no impact on the price of the stock. On the other hand, in a company with a very small market capitalization, the company is less visible and has little inertia. Each management member is regarded as essential to the operation of the company, and sales by management are viewed as a lack of confidence in the company's future. Therefore, it is very difficult for management of a small company to sell stock.

The marketplace is much less sensitive to sales by the venture capitalist, because once a company goes public, venture capitalists are not viewed as essential any longer to the business operations. The shareholders that have bought stock in the IPO are not counting on the venture capitalist to run the business. The marketplace is relatively insensitive to venture capitalists selling, because investors understand that sales are essential to the conduct of the venture capital business.

Valuation and Negotiations

When selling in an acquisition, you want the highest price you can get, consistent with leaving the company in good shape and in good hands. Historical data usually exists that enables you to see when valuations are relatively high or low according to standard metrics as adjusted for current company and economic conditions. It is usually not too difficult to see where one is in terms of the valuation cycle.

It is a different story when you are taking a company public. When a company wants to raise additional capital through a follow-on offering, it is important that the buyers of the IPO made money. A public company will probably be granting equity incentives to employees and needs to have a rising stock. A company should not seek to go public at its all time high price and never have it sell at that price again. When taking the company public, it is not necessarily bad business to leave something on the table in terms of price. And, of course, if the venture capitalist plans to distribute or liquidate interests once the lockup period is over, he would like the price of the stock to be higher rather than lower after the offering.

In regard to company valuation, it is not beneficial to have a unique perception of value. If the perception of value is not shared by the marketplace, then it blocks a sale, unless the sale is totally necessary. A seller has to be realistic. When selling a company, the venture capitalist needs to understand how the marketplace values that company.

The venture capitalist might decide that the market does not appreciate certain aspects of the company, and that he has superior insight as to its potential. If the venture capitalist's perception of value is lower than that of the marketplace, that is a good time to sell. If his perception of value is higher than that of the marketplace, he may decide to wait, if he has no better use for the capital or no external reason for the sale.

When looking for a good buyer, the venture capitalist searches for a buyer that has assets that his company does not have so the buyer can add value to his company. Once again, the guiding principle for a venture capitalist should be to help a company to achieve its long-term economic potential.

After identifying the logical buyers, the seller should determine who the decision makers are and the appropriate channels through which to approach them. A large company that is active in acquisitions usually has someone well identified as the contact person. Selling is, at times, a more subtle process. The seller may get a better price if the acquirer perceives the transaction as his idea rather than the seller's. Seeds can be planted in subtle ways, by entering into business discussions ostensibly unrelated to a potential sale. Intermediaries can also be effective in bringing information to the potential buyer. Even if your company has made the decision to sell and has identified three logical buyers, you might need to approach each of the three differently.

You always want to have competing buyers, but at some point you may have to sign an exclusive agreement, because an acquiring company may not be willing to commence due diligence work if there is a potential of a bidding war. But from the seller's point of view, there should be at least tacit understanding that other buyers are waiting in the wings. The seller is unlikely to get the best price if the acquirer believes there are no alternatives. One of the alternatives can be taking the company public if the seller does not get the price it wants. A company may even go public, let the public market determine valuation, and then use that valuation as a means of establishing an appropriate price.

If the company cannot find a buyer and the company is in trouble, it is imperative to reduce the burn rate. The company should economize wherever possible, while retaining the key employees that are needed to sell the assets with the employees that are critical to ongoing value attached. The venture capitalist should strive to hold the business together to make the most orderly disposition and achieve the best result possible under the adverse circumstances. The venture capitalist may have to establish special incentives so that key employees will stay throughout the process.

Exit Strategy Mistakes

Being unrealistic about the value of a company is a major mistake. So, too, is being overly eager or overly aggressive, and trying to force a sale. The biggest mistake of all is greed – not realizing that the timing of a sale is much more important than trying to get the absolute last nickel. The windows of opportunity for a good exit are fleeting, and if the venture capitalist misses a window, it may turn a big win into a complete loss.

Greed can lead to the value of the company never being realized. Shopping a deal in the interest of greed is also a mistake; word often gets out when a company has been shopped around. Potential buyers like to feel that a potential deal is a valuable and special opportunity. If a company is being shopped, the connotation is that many people have passed on it, which tarnishes its perceived value.

Another common mistake is that management has an unrealistic expectation about its future role in the company. If management puts its own career interests ahead of shareholders' interests, the company may not get sold at all.

How Careful Planning Enters Into Exits

Investment bankers offer the classic advice: "When the geese are quacking, feed them." The same message is conveyed by "Strike while the iron is hot." Both adages convey the wisdom that timing is the most important consideration in an exit.

It pays to be patient, not greedy. The actual price the seller is going to get is determined by the market; to establish a market, the seller needs competing buyers. As long as there are competing buyers and the timing is propitious, the seller should get the lion's share of realistic value. Negotiating beyond realistic value is not wise, because it leads to missing the window of opportunity to sell. Beyond a point, hard bargaining can well result in missing the market.

Careful planning and a good sense of timing are essential to realizing fair value in the sale of a healthy business with any exit strategy. The venture capitalist should always be mindful that he is in business for the long haul and let his sale decisions, as well as his investment decisions, be guided by the North Star of doing what will help the investee company realize its full potential.

Charles E. Harris is Chairman and CEO of Harris & Harris Group since 1984. He has served as a director, trustee, control person, chairman and/or chief executive officer of various publicly and privately held corporations and not-for-profit institutions.

Prior to 1984, he was Chairman of Wood, Struthers and Winthrop Management Corp., the investment advisory subsidiary of Donaldson, Lufkin & Jenrette. He was a member of the Advisory Panel for the Congressional Office of Technology Assessment. He is a member of the New York Society of Security Analysts.

Among his eleemosynary activities, he is currently a Trustee of Cold Spring Harbor Laboratory, a private not-for-profit institution that conducts research and education programs in the fields of molecular biology and genetics; a Trustee of the Nidus Center, a life sciences business incubator in St. Louis, Missouri; and a life-sustaining fellow of the Massachusetts Institute of Technology and a Shareholder of its Entrepreneurship Center.

He graduated from Princeton University (A.B., 1964) and Columbia University Graduate School of Business (MBA, 1967).

VC Exit Strategies in a Back to Basics Economy

Frédéric Veyssière

Partner
Innovacom

Investment Holding

There are three main stages for venture capital investments: early stage, mid-stage and late stage. If you invest in a company at the late stage, when the company already has revenue and possibly positive cash flow, then your holding of the investment will be much shorter than the typical timeline of five to seven years for early stage investors. By early stage we mean a company with about ten people who have been working on a project for about a year, bootstrapping the company. It is important to note, however, that the time to exit was considerably shortened during the recent high-tech bubble that occurred between 1999 and 2001.

A few years ago, there was much hype about service providers – for example, the telephone companies expanding their networks and installing more and more fiber optics and optical systems. At that time major players bought out companies quickly – within 1.5-2 years. JDS Uniphase or Cisco, for example, bought billions of dollars of component or system start-up companies with very little commercial traction. Because the market was soaring, the cost of the acquisition was rapidly dwarfed by the increase in valuation for the acquirers. The duration of the exiting position for VCs was dramatically reduced to one-and-a-half to two years, even for early stage investors!

In today's healthy business plan, the growth is much more gradual – typically over a four to six year period. Five to seven years is a good exiting time for the typical early stage investor, although the appetite of the market in a given sector can always change that timeframe.

The general economy is, of course, an important factor for exit timing. It is difficult right now for VCs in the technology sector to find decent exits for their companies. The acquisition of a competitor can trigger further assessment of whether it is a good time to exit.

There are two main ways to exit an investment: merger or acquisition (M&A) and initial public offering (IPO).

The M&A Process

We decide on an *ad hoc* basis when to go through an M&A, and we don't always follow the same procedure each time, though there are some consistent steps.

Typically we, the board of directors of the company, hire an investment banker who, with company management and maybe the board of directors, puts together a short list of potential acquirers. The banker presents the company to the potential acquirers on the list, playing the role of intermediary. When the demand is strong, we narrow the list to one or two potential acquirers – obviously it's better to have two companies looking at the acquisition as it drives the price up.

A good strategic buyer is one that gets to a better competitive position in its own market after the acquisition. Usually the management of the company seeking a buyer knows best its strategic positioning and who is likely to be a most suitable buyer.

During the due diligence process, suitable acquirers look carefully at the technology, the management team, and the market potential. At the end of the due diligence process, an offer is usually put on the table. Again, it's better for us if two offers are made, as they improve our bargaining position in the negotiations.

There are many ways to value a company. In the end, it is a matter of negotiation, the market appetite, and how our company will help the acquirer become more competitive in its own market. The company may have more value for one acquirer than another acquirer. In the end, the price will be the result of negotiations between the management team, the investment bankers on both sides, and the acquirer.

If a company has run out of cash, has no additional funding strategies, and is forced to sell, its options are very limited and usually go to liquidation or bankruptcy. Management and investors get very little of the proceeds in a liquidation or bankruptcy, since most of the proceeds go to cover liquidation costs. A far more attractive option is to merge with another company with which there is a strategic fit.

The IPO Process

If an IPO is possible, we will usually go with an IPO over an M&A because, over the long run, an IPO yields higher returns for the investor. In recent years IPOs have been rare, so the exit strategy has been mostly M&A.

To consider doing an IPO, a company needs to have a very predictable revenue growth and a minimum of three consecutive quarters of positive cash flow.

Usually, the company hires an investment banker, who talks to the VCs, company management – the CEO, the CFO, and perhaps other C-level executives – and other board members to form a picture of expectations.

The investment banker – not the VCs or the management team – determines how much of the company will be offered to the public. Typically, the portion offered is between 10 percent and 50 percent of the company. The percentage of the company to be offered to the public is usually determined based on the amount of money the company wants to raise and the valuation of the company.

Comparables in the industry – similar companies that have been sold in the past six months to one year – are the most widely used tools to set a valuation range. The final valuation depends on the market demand for the company. Discounted cash flow methods are also another tool used to establish a valuation.

The investment banker prepares a memorandum on the company describing what it has been doing and plans to do. The private placement memorandum is extremely precise: it includes all of the company's plans for the next five years, noting the markets to be targeted and the new product offerings. To support that plan, the memorandum will come up with an appropriate amount of money the company needs to raise. Also, market valuation will decide how much of the company needs to be sold to the public. For example, if the company is valued at $150 million and needs to raise $50 million, the company will have to sell one third of its shares to the public.

Six months after the IPO (lockup period), VCs will usually sell their share. IPOs are preferred exit strategies for VCs because most of the time they yield a higher market return than M&As.

Market Conditions Needed for Best Valuation

Even with adverse market conditions, M&As can sometimes produce decent returns. For example, if a large company believes it is strategically advantageous to buy your company to augment their portfolio of products and services, they will proceed with the purchase even though market conditions may be poor. M&As will also tend to occur in bad market conditions, where companies tend to have lower valuations that make acquisitions more attractive.

IPOs, on the other hand, need good market conditions. A company considering an IPO needs to make sure there is a strong demand for that type of company on the market. The investment banker usually sets the agenda and decides on the timing of an IPO.

Deciding on the Valuation

The most highly utilized tool in deciding on a company valuation is to compare it with similar companies operating in the same sector. The investment banker will usually research all the comparable companies that have been sold in the past 6-12 months and come up with a list of ratios. Ratios equal value of the company and its significant indicator; a significant indicator could be sales, net income, cash flow, etc.

For each company, the following types of ratios are calculated: value as a multiple of revenue, as a multiple of earnings before tax depreciation and amortization (EBITDA), as a multiple of net income, or as a multiple of free cash flow. All these ratios are averaged out and an approximate valuation is derived for our company. However, the actual final number that will be inked on the term sheet is the result of negotiation between the parties involved.

Negotiations are very specific to the deal. One of the most important elements needed for a company to get best terms for its sale is to have two acquirers, which puts the company in a competitive bidding situation. When times were better in the technology sector, a competing offer to an M&A was quite often an IPO. This allowed the company to elevate the bidding substantially.

When a Company Is Forced to Sell

If a company runs out of cash, a decision must be made to determine its future. This situation has occurred with increasing frequency in the last few years, especially with technology companies. The question for VCs, then, becomes whether to invest more money in the company and see if the market opens up later on or to shut down the company.

If it appears the market is unlikely to open up in the next few years, the VC has to decide whether to pull the plug on the company or not.

First, the VC tries to sell the assets of company, especially in the high technology sector because those companies still have intellectual property, such as patents. Although they may not have customers, they do have value. It is difficult to get a good price, though, but the goal is always to get the best price possible.

The second option, which may be considered in parallel with the first, is to look for a merger opportunity. For example, in the fiber optics sector, four or five companies would go after the same market with slightly different technologies. There is usually not room for all of them. A natural consolidation can therefore happen in the market as two companies get together and become stronger as one. Perhaps one company has cash, and the other has intellectual property, and their merger benefits both. There is usually a recapitalization, where all investors of the merger agree to put cash back into the new company. The negotiation centers on how much the stock of one company is worth for the other company.

When it is not possible to follow either of these options, the only real alternative is to liquidate the company.

Purchase Price and Returns

When the purchase price is above the overall amount invested in the company, calculating returns for the investors is simple. There are two types of stock: common and preferred. When the price is well above the last round of financing, everyone's interest is usually converted to common stock. A price per share is calculated, and everyone is given money based on his or her number of shares.

When the purchase price is below the company's last round valuation, not everyone will receive their money back.

Let's look at a simple example to illustrate how it works.

Usually there are a few successive rounds of funding. The first round of funding is called Series A. At the end of the first round of funding, you have Preferred A stock and common stock. The second round of funding is called Series B. At the end of the second round, you have common stock, Preferred Series A stock, and Preferred Series B stock. The third round of funding is called Series C, at the end of which you have common stock, Preferred Series A stock, Preferred Series B stock, and Preferred Series C stock. Preferred stockholders are paid before common stockholders. Within the preferred stock, usually Series C gets paid before Series B and Series A. Preferred stock is held by investors. Company management and employees typically hold common stock.

If the company's last round of funding, let's say Series C funding, raised $10 million, Series C has a liquidation preference of 1X, which means that when there is an exit, they have to equal one times their investment before everyone else gets paid. So if there were an acquisition of the company for $10 million, the $10 million would go to Series C Preferred stockowners. Series A and Series B Preferred stock owners and owners of common stock would receive no payment.

If the company is acquired for $20 million, Series C will receive the first $10 million because they have the 1X liquidation preference. The remaining $10 million depends on the liquidation preferences of Series B and Series A. Normally, Series B would receive the remaining $10 million, and Series A Preferred and common would receive no payment. Although there is always a standard term sheet, there could be major variation regarding these terms depending on the bargaining power of the investors vs. the company. For example, the standard liquidation preference is 1X but 2X, 3X and even 5X liquidation preferences can also occur!

With a low acquisition price, the common stockholders will usually receive nothing in a sale. That is the reason why some of the acquisition price– about 10 percent– is usually set aside for the founders and management. This way, it keeps the management interested and motivated in helping the company be successful in the future.

Common Entrepreneur Exit Mistakes

The board makes the exit decision. Entrepreneurs are part of the board, but not the only board members. Most entrepreneur mistakes revolve around the timing of the exit

Sometimes the entrepreneurs want to sell too early. They have sold the company and later learn the market is expanding much more than expected and they could have sold the company for a larger sum.

Another mistake made by entrepreneurs is refusing to sell at a given price because they think they can get a better valuation in the future. It could be a risky bet as the market can rapidly turn down.

The most common mistakes made by entrepreneurs regarding exits are being too shortsighted or too farsighted, thereby missing the optimal time to sell the company.

Best Venture Capital Advice

Early stage venture capital is not about quick return on investments. If market conditions allow that, so much the better. But early stage VC is actually a long-term business.

Being a VC is quite different from being a trader on the stock market. VCs have to focus on building great companies – a robust company with strong products and customer focus– and preferably strong barriers to entry making it very difficult to copy.

The best advice for VCs is to focus on building great companies, rather than focusing on when the liquidity will come. As great companies are being built, exit options will always come in time. Wall Street always recognizes good strong companies with healthy cash flows and the IPO door will open up when the time is right.

Sometimes the management team merely wants to prepare the company for a quick acquisition. This often worked during the tech bubble, but is less likely to work in the current market. We are back to basics, where it's best to build a sustainable business for the long term. I would recommend solely focusing on building a good company and forgetting about a potential M&A or IPO. A healthy company will sooner or later be presented with interesting exit strategies.

Golden Rules for Successful VC Exits

VCs should focus on helping grow a strong company and working hard with the management team to reach that goal. Even though VCs may feel some pressure from investors for liquidity, they should continue to focus on building a healthy company. This is a long-term investment of over five to seven years of consistent hard work.

In today's economy, companies are back to basics: they can only survive if they build real value. During the tech bubble, we saw many companies collapsing a few months after their IPOs. It is now much more difficult for companies to do IPOs. However, companies that can make it will be much stronger in the long run.

Based in San Francisco, California, Frédéric joined Innovacom in 2000. His major investments include Actelis Networks, Aperto Networks, Atrica and Metconnex.

Prior to joining Innovacom in 2000, Frédéric worked with TeleSoft Partners, a San Mateo–based venture capital fund, as a consultant in charge of business development for Europe. From 1992 to 1999, Frédéric was director, then vice president of Business Development & Operations with France Telecom North America in New York, heading several key projects including the implementation of the company's Internet backbone in the US, the investment of France Telecom in Sprint PCS, and the business planning and implementation in the U.S. of the first gateway allowing seamless roaming between GSM-900 and DCS-1900 networks. Prior to joining France Telecom in 1992, Frédéric was an associate in the M&A Group of La Compagnie Financière Edmond de Rothschild in Paris focusing on telecom and IT transactions.

Frédéric holds an MS in physics from Paris Science University, magna cum laude; an MS in telecommunications engineering from the École Nationale Supérieure des Télécommunications in Paris; and an MBA from the Columbia Graduate School of Business.

VC FORUM

THE QUARTERLY JOURNAL Where Leaders INTERACT

Trying to stay a step ahead of the key issues every venture capital professional needs to be aware of? Interested in interacting with a community of senior venture capitalists, entrepreneurs and executives from the world's top firms? For only $219.95 a year, subscribe today to VC Forum, the quarterly journal for the senior most intelligence with respect to the venture capital business.

Sample VC Forum and Aspatore Published Authors Include:

Michael Moritz, Partner, Sequoia Capital
Heidi Roizen, Partner, Softbank
David J. Cowan, GP, Bessemer Venture Partners
Anthony Sun, Co-CEO & Managing General Partner, Venrock
Mark Anson, Chief Investment Officer, CalPERS
Lawrence E. Mock, Jr., President & CEO, Mellon Ventures, Inc.
Terry McGuire, Co-Founder & Managing General Partner, Polaris
Graham Anderson, General Partner, EuclidSR Partners
Oliver D. Curme, General Partner, Battery Ventures
Jonathan Goldstein, Partner, TA Associates
Suzanne King, Partner, New Enterprise Associates
Mathias Schilling, Partner, Bertelsmann Ventures
Michael Carusi, GP, Advanced Technology Ventures
Mark Macenka, Testa Hurwitz & Thiebeault, Business Chair
Patrick Ennis, Arch Venture Partners, Partner
Gerard DiFiore, Reed Smith, Corporate Group Head
Sam Colella, Versant Ventures, Managing Director
Robert Chefitz, Apax Partners, General Partner

VC Forum is a quarterly journal that enables professionals connected to venture capital to cover all their knowledge bases and participate as a member of a community of leading executives. VC Forum is an interactive journal, the content of which is provided exclusively by its readership, and upon subscribing, new members become eligible to submit articles for possible publication in the journal. While other venture related resources focus on current events, specific industries, or funded deals, VC Forum helps professionals stay one step ahead of major venture related trends that are occurring 3 to 6 months from now.

With only 24 hours in a day, venture related professionals are expected to have a sound understanding of every aspect of the business, be aware of all major economic trends, and keep up with constant changes in the corporate world as a whole – a task that would be impossible without the appropriate resources. Each quarterly issue features articles on the core areas of which every venture related professional must be aware, in order to stay one step ahead - including trends in valuations, management teams, governance, exit strategies, M&A, tax and legal strategies, and more. Over the course of the year, VC Forum features the thinking of executives from over half the top 250 leading venture capital firms, investors in venture capital funds, investment bankers, entrepreneurs from VC funded companies, legal and accounting venture capital related specialists around the world.

Other Best Sellers

Visit Your Local Bookseller Today or
www.Aspatore.com For More Information